Fundamentals of Buddhist Ethics

Fundamentals of
BUDDHIST ETHICS

Gunapala Dharmasiri

GOLDEN LEAVES, U.S.A.

Library of Congress
Cataloging in Publication Data:

Dharmasiri, Gunapala.
Fundamentals of Buddhist Ethics.

Bibliography: p.
Includes index.
ISBN 0-942353-02-1 (pbk.)
1. Buddhist ethics. 2. Buddhism--Doctrines.
I. Title.
BJ1289.D43 1989 87-36743
294.3'5--dc19 CIP

Published in the United States of America by

GOLDEN LEAVES PUBLISHING COMPANY
2190 WILBUR AVENUE
ANTIOCH, CALIFORNIA 94509

Typeset in the United States of America by
Golden Leaves Publishing Company

Manufactured in the United States of America

To
rahju and ranjeet

Contents

Foreword

We are passing through critical times. Although humanity has been pursuing the 'mirage' of progress, we have actually ended up in a chamber of horrors as the contemporary social situation amply shows. Mankind has morally deteriorated to an unprecedented extent while through communications and travel, the world has been reduced to a global village. Immorality is all too pervasive and increasingly virulent.

It is important to note that humanity has perpetrated some notable crimes in recent history, such as the killing of people in cold blood—terrorism (now part of the norm rather than exceptional); dictatorship of the patriarchy and the denial of equal rights to more than half of the human population—women, who perform perhaps the most arduous and significant task of humanity, child-bearing; the attempts of the powerful countries (adhering to the principle that 'might is right') to keep the weaker countries under perpetual slavery by exploiting them through all forms of subtle means, thus weakening them further and in the process condemning a part of our common planet to eternal damnation by calling it 'the Third World'; spending over three-fourths of our common wealth for programs to kill other human beings (warfare), while untold billions are slowly starving; the raping of nature and the treatment of animals as objects of food or fun; to name only a few.

Milan Kundera comments: "True human goodness, in all its purity and freedom, can come to the fore only when its recipient has no power. Mankind's true moral test, its fundamental test (which lies deeply buried from the view), consists of its attitude towards those who are at its mercy; animals. And in this respect mankind has suffered a fundamental debacle, a debacle so fundamental that all others stem from it." (Milan Kundera, *The Unbearable Lightness of Being*, Faber & Faber, London, 1984, p. 289).

Due to the diminuition of moral and spiritual values in human consciousness, there is a diminished awareness of the existence of such values. The only recognizable values left are the animalistic and instinctive drives of self-preservation and procreation. When human imagination magnifies these values, money and sex become our latest brand of religion. People just forget that we are humans, capable of much higher achievements. In this anomie of values, people have simply forgotten that there are other higher dimensions possible in life. Of course, some people see the desperate need to go beyond this tragic situation, but they do not have a clear conception of an alternative. It is interesting to read the comments of a modern writer, whose contemporary perspective perhaps retrospectively reflects much of the whole past history of humanity: "The important thing is that we get rid of the sexual hassles that have obsessed the human race since the dawn of civilization, that have totally dominated our music, our art, our literature, our conversations, our thoughts, our dreams, and our very souls, so we can get on with what we were really put on earth to do. Whatever the hell THAT is". ('Designer Genes', by Dave Barry, in *Ms.*, Sept. 1985, Vol. XIV. No. 3, p. 117).

It is definitely frightening to see humanity becoming desensitized and disintegrated in this way both morally and spiritually. In this desperate situation, where can we turn for help? Many religions have warned us about the coming of ages such as ours, and have also advised us that the only hope in such situations is to take refuge in morality, which is said to be capable of protecting us in every way.

What morality? It is here that we need enlightenment about what morality is. We must do away with the patriarchal and authoritarian morality. It is in this context that the Buddhist theory of morality can help us because, as one of the most universal and consistent systems of morality, it is based on a profound vision of reality. It is a morality coupled with wisdom.

This book is an attempt to treat Buddhist ethics, taking into account the whole spectrum of Buddhism from Theravada through Mahayana to Buddhist Tantra, avoiding the lamentable parochialism exhibited by many Buddhist scholars. It is also hoped that our treatment will show that Buddhist ethics cannot be satisfactorily analyzed through Western categories of ethical analysis (like teleology and deontology) because the basic Buddhist ethical principles are not at all amenable to narrow Western thought categories, Buddhist ethics being not merely an ethical theory but a teaching based on a profound vision of reality unheard of in Western traditions.

This morality, based on wisdom, may be our only refuge . . .

Dharmasiri

Acknowledgments

This book is partly based on a series of lectures given at Swarthmore College and Haverford College in the United States, during 1981-1982. I am thankful to the Fullbright Foundation for inviting me to the United States as Fullbright Visiting Professor to do these lectures. I am also thankful to Swarthmore College for honoring me with a Julian Cornell Visiting Professorship along with my Fullbright appointment, an arrangement that generated extra time for me to write this book.

It is with deep gratitude that I remember Donald Swearer, who in every way encouraged me to write this book; Patrick Henry, who taught me most generously how to handle the mighty computer at Swarthmore College, which I used to edit this book; Linwood Urban and Jacob Meskin for their suggestions after patiently going through the first draft; and Bruno Gujer for valuable editorial comments.

John, Tami, Nina and Laura, four Swarthmore students, who carefully looked after my family and me during my stay there, were a constant moral encouragement to me while I was engaged in this work.

I am indebted to my wife, Kusum, for dexterously managing the family during the period I was working on the book, and I am thankful to my daughter, Kanchuka, (the secret pass word to my computer files) and to my twin sons, Asanga and Vasubandhu, for kindly leaving me alone when I was engaged in thought constructions.

Finally, my gratitude to the Golden Leaves Publishing Company of California, for publishing this American edition.

Gunapala Dharmasiri

Department of Philosophy
Peradeniya University
Peradeniya, Sri Lanka

Abbreviations

A.	*Aṅguttara Nikāya*
A.A.	*Aṅguttara Nikāya Aṭṭhakathā, i.e. Monorathapūranī*
B.P.S.	Buddhist Publication Society
C.V.	*Culla Vagga*
D.	*Dīgha Nikāya*
D.A.	*Dīgha Nikāya Aṭṭhakathā, i.e. Sumangalavilāsinī*
Dhp.	*Dhammapada*
E.B.T.K.	Early Buddhist Theory of Knowledge
It.	*Itivuttaka*
J.	*Jātaka*
Kvu.	*Kathāvatthu*
M.	*Majjhima Nikāya*
M.A.	*Majjhima Nikāya Aṭṭakathā, i.e. Papañcasūdanī*
Netti.	*Nettippakarana*
Pa.	*Paramatthajotikā: Commentary on Sutta Nipāta*
PP.	The Path of Purification
P.T.S.	Pali Text Society
S.	*Saṃyutta Nikāya*
S.A.	*Saṃyutta Nikāya Aṭṭhakathā, i.e. Sāratthappakāsinī*
S.B.B.	Sacred Books of the Buddhists
Sn.	*Sutta Nipāta*
Th.	*Thera Gāthā*
U.	*Udāna*
Vsm.	*Visuddhimagga*

The Pali texts referred to are editions of the Pali Text Society, London.

1

Background To Buddhist Ethics

Gotama, the Buddha, was born in the sixth century B.C. as Prince Siddhartha, the heir to a kingdom. He had all conceivable luxuries and sensual enjoyments. But he was not happy. Because he saw the barren emptiness and meaninglessness in all the variety of luxuries around him, he felt that life was basically unsatisfactory. One day he secretly left the palace and the family and entered into a search for the ultimate happiness. Many religious thinkers of his day advocated the practice of austerity as a means of attaining this happiness and he tried this method rigorously for six years, but failed. Then he came to the conclusion that ultimate happiness could be found neither by sensual enjoyments nor by austerities. After abandoning these which he called 'the two extreme paths'[2] and following the 'middle path', he gained insight into the true nature of things, and became enlightened, or the Buddha. In this enlightenment, he realized that morality and wisdom were the two main paths for attaining the ultimate happiness or salvation.

He taught his findings as the *Dhamma*, meaning The Truth. Known as Early Buddhism, these teachings can be grouped under four headings: (1) Epistemology or theory of knowledge, (2) A cosmology of the universe and of the world, (3) A theory of morality, and (4) A theory of the ultimate reality or salvation called Nirvana. The main focus of this book is on the Buddhist account of morality, and in the last section we shall discuss the nature of Nirvana. As background for these moral and spiritual investigations, we will in this section briefly discuss the first two aspects of Buddhist philosophy.

Buddhist Theory of Knowledge

Buddhism is one of the most anti-authoritarian systems of thinking. The Buddha is against accepting any one or anything as an authority except oneself. He states this principle, which is unique in the history of human thinking, in the *Kālāma Sutta* as follows: "Now, look you Kālāmas, do not be led by reports, or tradition, or hearsay. Be not led by the authority of religious texts, nor by mere logic or speculative standpoints, nor by considering appearances, nor by the delight in speculative views, nor by seeming possibilities, nor by the idea: 'this is our teacher.' But, O Kālāmas, when you know for yourselves that certain things are unwholesome (*akusala*) and wrong and bad, then give them up . . . And when you know for yourselves that certain things are wholesome (*kusala*) and good, then accept them and follow them."[1]

Not only others' teachings, but, the Buddha said, his own teachings themselves should be subjected to careful scrutiny before acceptance. He went as far as saying that an inquiring monk should first examine the Buddha himself so as to verify whether his teaching is really enlightened before accepting him as the Buddha.[2] He did not claim any authority on the basis of omniscience, which he expressly rejected when others attributed it to him.[3] He took care not to allow any authoritarian tradition to enter into the Buddhist-fold after his death when he refused to nominate an authoritative person to succeed him and maintained that the only authority should be the *Dhamma*, which he himself regarded and respected as his own Teacher.

However, Buddhism has a conception of faith called *Saddhā*. The Buddha distinguishes two kinds of *Saddhā*, as ungrounded or irrational faith (*amūlikā saddhā*), which he condemns, and rational faith(*ākāravatī saddhā*)[4], advocating the usefulness of the latter which is similar to the faith a scientist reposes in a probable hypothesis that has to be verified. As a scientist leaves faith and obtains knowledge when his hypothesis is verified, a Buddhist, after attaining realization, becomes a person who has left faith behind (*as-saddho*).[5]

The Buddha also rejected *a priori* reasoning and abstract speculation as means of knowledge because, according to him, reasoning was only concerned with validity, not truth. Though a line of reasoning may be logically valid, it may not be factually true.

He even criticized accepting the majority view (*mahatī janatā*) as a dangerous criterion of truth because the majority could be wrong. Therefore, to a questioner who tried to base an argument on the strength of the acceptance by the majority, the Buddha said that he should form his own opinion about things rather than being led by others' opinions.[7]

The Buddha maintained that one must neither accept nor reject an idea because of one's likes or dislikes, without proper investigation. Until the idea is verified, one must temporarily safeguard it (*saccānurakkhaṇa*)[8], because what one might reject, might turn out, after all, to be true.

He accepted perception and inference as the two basic means of knowledge and based the principle of inference on the law of causality. With regard to perception, he also accepted, as means of knowledge, extrasensory forms of perception like telepathy and clairaudience and stated that anyone could attain these extrasensory powers through meditational exercises.[9]

The Buddha said that many unnecessary philosophical problems arise due to the confused nature of our concepts and language, and therefore advocated clarity in thinking and use of language. He called himself an analyst (*vibhajjāvado'haṃ nāhaṃ ekaṃsavādo*)[10] and said that not every question can be categorically answered (*i.e.* in a straight-forward manner). According to the Buddha, there are four types of questions: (1) Some questions can be categorically answered (*ekaṃsa-vyākaraṇīya*). If someone asks whether the world is impermanent, one can categorically say 'yes'. (2) Some questions should be first analyzed before answering (*vibhajja-vyākaraṇīya*): If a person asks whether by doing volitional actions one goes to a good birth, one should say that volitional acts can be divided into two types, good and bad, and say that while good volitional acts lead one to good births, the opposite acts lead to bad births. (3) To answer some questions, one must first question the questioner (*paṭipucchā-vyākaraṇīya*): If someone asks whether a particular person is tall or short, we must question the questioner, 'in relation to whom?'. (4) There are some questions that cannot be answered at all (*ṭhapanīya*) because they involve mistakes of category: When a flame blows out, if someone asks, 'to which direction did the flame go'; it cannot be answered because there was no 'thing' called the flame to start with.

The Buddha further classified questions into meaningful (*sappaṭihīrakataṃ pañhaṃ*) and meaningless (*appaṭihīrakataṃ pañhaṃ*)[11] and stated the principle of verification as the criterion of meaning. If a person says that 'I am building a staircase to climb up to a mansion' but fails to show where the mansion is, or if he cannot show how the existence of the mansion can be verified through experience, then his statement becomes meaningless. Thus the Buddha's epistemological approach was empirical and anti-metaphysical. He also cautioned that in using language, we should not overstretch concepts by taking them beyond their conventional usage (*samaññaṃ nātidhāveyya*).[12]

As a further step towards clarity in the use of language, he used a four-fold system of logic[13] which goes beyond the standard two alternatives of 'is' and 'is not'. The third alternative, 'is *and* is not' was not meant to be a contradiction but a statement of an existing state of affairs. For example, in classifying the theories prevalent in his time about the extent of the world, the Buddha used this third alternative to state the view that maintained "the world is finite in one direction (*i.e.* vertically) and infinite in another direction (*i.e.* horizontally)." The fourth alternative of 'neither is nor is not' is applicable to theories that maintain that epithets like the 'finite' and 'infinite' are not applicable to a situation such as that of the world. Thus, by facilitating more precise forms of expression, the four-fold system of Early Buddhist logic helps to increase clarity of language and its expressions.

The Buddha accepted correspondence with facts (*yathābhūta*)[14] as the criterion as well as the nature of truth, and regards coherence as the nature of truth. However, the Buddha applied important pragmatic criteria in deciding which truths we must investigate. We must investigate only those truths that are existentially relevant to our moral and spiritual search. He said that human life is too short and therefore too precious to waste time in groping after useless truths, and that instead, we should devote our full attention to finding out the truths that will lead us out of our existential predicament. As an example, he says that if a person is shot with an arrow, he should not first try to discover the direction from which the arrow came or the person who shot the arrow, but be fully concerned about removing the arrow and attending to the wound.

The Buddhist Concept of the Universe and the World

The Buddha had two conceptions of the world. One was of the external objective world, and the other of the 'personal world'. His understanding of the objective world is in the context of the universe. The universe is understood in terms of a vast cosmic space.

G. P. Malalasekara and K. N. Jayatilleke summarize the Buddha's view: "In this vastness of cosmic space are located an innumerable number of worlds. As far as these suns and moons revolve, shedding their light in space, so far extends the thousand-fold world-system. In it are a thousand suns, a thousand moons, thousands of earths and thousands of heavenly worlds. This is said to be the thousand-fold minor world-system. A thousand times such a thousand-fold minor world-system is the twice-a-thousand middling world-system. A thousand times such a twice-a-thousand middling world-system is the twice-a-thousand major world system."[15] Malalasekara and Jayatilleke identify these systems with the galactic systems. The Buddha states his conception: "As far as moons and suns move in their course and light up all quarters with their radiance, so far extends the thousand-fold world-system. Therein are a thousand moons, a thousand suns, a thousand *Sinerus*, lords of mountains, a thousand Rose-Apple Lands, a thousand Western Ox-Wains, a thousand Northern Kurus, a thousand Eastern Videhas; four thousand Mighty Oceans, four thousand Mighty Rulers, a thousand Four Great Rulers, a thousand heavens of the Thirty-three, a thousand Yama worlds, a thousand heavens of the *Devas* of Delight, a thousand heavens of the *Devas* that delight in creation, the same of those *Devas* that delight in Others' Creations, and a thousand Brahma worlds. This, Ananda, is called "The system of the thousand lesser worlds." A system a thousand-fold the size of this is called "The Twice-a-Thousand Middling Thousand-fold World-system." A system a thousand-fold the size of this is called "The Thrice-a-thousand Mighty Thousand-fold World-system."[16] And the Buddha says that the universe extends even further. These galactic systems are always subject to change internally and externally. Externally, these are in the process of contraction and expansion (*samvaṭṭamāna*) and (*vivaṭṭamāna*). This idea is similar to the modern theory of the oscillating universe. "But the time, we are told, is not the same everywhere, for fifty earth years are equivalent to one day and night in one of the heavenly worlds, while in another a day and night is equivalent to no less than 1,600 years."[17] "The span of life of mortal men is insignificantly small in comparison with cosmic time and may be compared in its duration to a line drawn in water."[18] There are varieties of beings living in these world-systems. "Several attempts are made to classify this vast array of beings. One such classification speaks of human beings, as well as some of the higher and lower beings, as falling into the class of beings who are different and distinguishable from each other in mind and body. There are other classes where the beings are different in body but one in mind. Yet others are alike in body but different in mind, while there are some who are alike both in body and in mind. A further set of four classes of beings are mentioned who are formless. All these are described as the several stations which the human consciousness can attain (*viññanaṭṭhiti*), and find renewed existence after death. Another such classification puts beings into the several classes of the "no-footed, the two-footed, the four-footed, the many-footed, those having or lacking material form, the conscious, the unconscious and the super-conscious. The human worlds are always represented as standing midway in the hierarchy of worlds. Life in these human worlds is a mixture of the pleasant and the unpleasant, the good and the evil, while the pleasant and good traits are intensified in the higher worlds and the unpleasant and evil in the lower."[19]

It is in terms of this infinite vast cosmic context that Buddhism tries to understand the place of man in the universe. In that context, man seems to be so small and insignificant, minuter than even the minutest dust, that he becomes less than nothing.

But, in this cosmic context, humans assume a unique position because we have the most rare privilege of easy accessibility to salvation. This is for two reasons. One is, as mentioned above, human worlds are a balanced mixture of pleasure and pain. When either the pleasure or the pain becomes intensified, one's mind does not easily turn toward spirituality. The other is the shortness of human life, and the unpredictability of the time of death. In other non-human worlds, the time scales are fairly high. Once you are born in them, you are bound to spend your quota of time allotted to you by your karma. Therefore, Buddhism regards the fact that we die relatively soon as an advantage and a privilege. We are propelled towards spirituality by the fear of imminent death.

Although the Buddha talked about our cosmic context, he discouraged cosmic speculations because such speculations have no existential relevance for us. Such speculations lead only to 'views'. Therefore, he strongly criticized such theories that maintained that the world was finite or infinite, *etc.* Addressing Vaccha, the Buddha comments: "The world is finite . . . this Vaccha, is going to a (speculative) view, holding a view, the wilds of views, the wriggling of views, the scuffling of views, the fetter of views; it is accompanied by anguish, distress, misery, fever; it does not conduce to turning away from, nor to dispassion, stopping, calming, super-knowledge, awakening, nor to *Nibbāna.* I, Vaccha, beholding that this is a peril, thus do not approach any of these views."[20]

Therefore, what is existentially relevant for us is not an understanding of this vast objective world, but our 'personal' world where we live, enjoy and suffer. The Buddha maintained that each one of us lives in one's own personal world, personally created by oneself, using one's own concepts. Therefore, the Buddha redefines the concept of the world and says that in his teachings the world is indistinguishable from the concept thereof. It is with this world that we should be concerned. He discusses the nature of this world: "That by which one is conscious of the world, by which one has conceit of the world—that is called 'world' in the Noble One's discipline. And through what is one conscious of the world? Through the eye, friends, through the ear, the nose, the tongue, the body and the mind . . . "[21] "That end of the world wherein one is not born, does not grow old or die or pass away or reappear, that, I declare, is impossible to be know, seen or reached by travelling. But, friend, I do not declare that one can make an end of suffering without reaching the end of the world. Friend, I do proclaim that in this very fathom-long body, with its perceptions and consciousness, is the world, the world's arising, the world's cessation and the path leading to the world's cessation."[33] " 'The world, the world', O Lord, they call it. In what sense, O Lord, is there a world or a concept of the world?" "Wherever, Samiddhi, there is the eye, the visible forms, the visual consciousness and the things perceptible with the visual consciousness, there is the world or the concept of it . . . wherever there is the ear . . . nose . . . tongue . . . body . . . mind . . . Wherever, Samiddhi, there is no eye, no visible forms, no visual consciousness and nothing perceptible with the visual consciousness, there is neither a world nor a concept of a world . . . Wherever there is no ear . . . nose . . . tongue . . . body . . . mind . . . "[23]

Ñāṇananda comments: "Thus the world is what our senses present it to us to be. However, the world is not purely a projection of the mind in the sense of a thoroughgoing idealism;[24] only, it is a phenomenon which the empirical consciousness cannot get behind, as it is itself committed to it. One might, of course, transcend the empirical consciousness and see the world objectively in the light of wisdom (*Pañña*) only to find that it is void (*suñña*) of the very characteristics which made it a 'world' for him."[25]

Three Basic Features of the World

There are three basic features that are common to all these worlds. They are called the basic truths of the world. We suffer in Samsara (the phenomenal cycle of existence) because we have not fully realized these three truths. Our Samsaric life is based on three basic assumptions which are completely false, therefore grounded in falsity or ignorance (*moha*). Our first assumption is that there are really existing non-changing objects in the world (*nicca*). The second is that persons and objects exist as independent substances (*atta*). The third is that we can achieve happiness in this worldly life (*sukha*). The three basic Buddhist truths are exactly the opposites of these three assumptions.

The first truth is impermanence (*anicca*), which means that everything, physical and mental, is in an everchanging flux. The second truth is non-substantiality (*anatta*) or that nothing has a soul or a substance. Through the process of conceptual projection, we conceptually freeze the flowing series and artificially fabricate objects. But all those objects are only parts of ever changing processes. As the Buddhist doctrine of Dependent Origination (*paṭiccasamuppāda*) emphasizes, everything arises and exists in relation to everything else. In other words, as the Mahayanists say, everything interpenetrates everything else. In this web of interdependence, a place for any kind of soul or substance disappears. Or, if we look at the same thing from another standpoint, everything can be analyzed until it is reduced to nothing. So, what 'really' exists is this 'nothingness'. The other side of the picture is the 'I'. It is 'I' who desires and suffers. Does this 'I' exist? If you look into yourself you will never find this 'I'. Buddha analyzed a person into five factors, form (*rūpa*), feelings (*vedanā*), sensations (*saññā*), dispositions (*saṃkhāra*), and consciousness (*viññaṇa*), and said that one could not find any unchanging principle like a self or a soul in any of them. If so, how do we get this feeling of 'I'? It is an illusion, a result of conceptualization. As we conceptualize and make outside objects through projection, we get the idea of a self in relation to the conceptual-world-building process. If we see a moving train while sitting in a stationary train, we think our train is moving. Likewise, in relation to the conceptual projections we make onto the external world, we tend to see an 'I'. If we stop these conceptual projections, the 'I' will vanish instantly.[26] Still another way of making the idea of *Anatta* meaningful is to consider the place of man and other things in the context of the vast cosmic space. Viewed in that perspective, man, or, for that matter, anything, gets reduced to a point of nothing.

The third truth is that this world or Samsaric life is basically suffering (*dukkha*). *Dukkha* is a term with wide connotations, ranging from gross physical suffering to subtle mental restlessness. The Buddha emphasized by this term that human life is ultimately non-satisfying. In our search for happiness, we jump from one goal to another in a desperate search for satisfaction or happiness. The farther we go, the farther away lies happiness. The Buddha said, "everyone dies with something lacking, there is no satisfaction in worldly pleasures" (*Ūnāva hutvāna jahanti dehaṃ, kāmehi lokamhi na hi atthi titti*). The Buddhist analysis tries to show that there is a paradox and a contradiction involved in worldly happiness. We achieve happiness by obtaining things which we consider valuable. Something becomes valuable to us in terms of conceptually-created value systems. Also, the value of a thing is proportionate to its unavailability. The more unavailable a thing is, the more valuable it is. And we think that if we obtain it we will be happy. But, the irony is, as soon as we achieve our goal, it becomes available. Although we may become temporarily excited and momentarily happy about our achievement, we soon forget about it and project our concepts to another thing and make it another goal and start running after it. At some point in this process of running, we suddenly die, without ever achieving our goal of happiness. All we had done was to run after a mirage. That was why the Buddha said that there is no meaning or essence in worldly life (*asāra*). Thus, worldly happiness is supposed to come, from achieving something that is unavailable. But, ironically, as soon as something is achieved, its unavailability disappears, and along with it, by definition, its value also disappears. With the erosion of the value, happiness gradually disappears. Therefore, worldly happiness is a contradiction in terms, because it can never be achieved. It is a logical impossibility.

The Buddha, of course, said that there are many kinds of worldly happiness. But he said that they are only temporary periods of excitement. It is these temporary periods, he said, which unfortunately create the false impression that happiness is available somewhere in this worldly life. But such excitements are very short-lived, and are essentially dependent on a prior period of deprivation and therefore 'conditioned'. Although these periods of excitement are rare, the continuous search for them keeps one tired and worried and full of anguish and anxiety. The Buddha refers to this basic underlying non-satisfaction in worldly life as *Dukkha*. He equates worldly happiness to a pleasure one gets from scratching an itch. Although it is a pleasure, it is dependent on pain. He said that when a person is completely cured of the itch, he enjoys a higher kind of happiness transcending the former dependent and short-lived pleasures, and that happiness he equates with Nirvanic bliss.

Therefore, the Buddha's central problem was how to get out of this unsatisfying Samsara and achieve a permanent kind of happiness. The path he found to cross Samsara consists of two aspects: morality and wisdom. It is wisdom (*paññā*) concerning ultimate reality or Nirvana that frees one from Samsara because it is ignorance (*moha*) that binds one to it. But this practice of wisdom must necessarily be coupled with the practice of morality, because the nature of Nirvana, or ultimate reality, is moral. Therefore, the practice of morality is a cultivation of Nirvanic features which will take one towards Nirvana. In other words, the practice of morality leads to enlightening results.

2

Motivation In Buddhist Ethics

There are some interesting issues that are specific to the Buddhist theory of ethics. These issues originate from the nature of the Buddhist theory of reality. A person does not have a self or a soul and is said to be made up of five factors. When these five factors come together, they constitute the person, just as a chariot is made up of the parts that constitute it. And, it is further said that these five factors are incessantly changing or are always in a sate of flux. In this state of affairs, can one meaningfully speak of 'a person'? If there is no person, there are problems for moral discourse, because ethical discourse presupposes the notions of 'personal responsibility', 'personal identity', 'personal initiative' and 'moral commitment'.

One could imagine these problems easily solved if we were to accept the theory of a self. But for the Buddha, the idea of a self could not be made meaningful in any way. The only way to make the idea of self meaningful is to verify it, and if we look at ourselves objectively in order to verify it, all we see is the above five factors. And if we introspect and subjectively look for a self, all we see is an ever changing series of thoughts and sensations. Therefore, if the idea of self or soul is not meaningful, we will have to explain things with the help of existing facts.

Although Buddhism does not accept the idea of a person as an enduring entity, it accepts the existence of a person as a composite of factors. Two criteria are used in determining the identity of a person. A person is made up of two types of groups of events, physical and mental. As all these groups are ever changing, the preceding events disappear, giving birth to succeeding events. Thus the succeeding events inherit the characteristics of the preceding events. This results in a causal sequence of events. In Buddhism, it is through this 'unbroken continuity or coherence of the series of events' (*avicch-inna santati sāmaggi*—Buddhaghosa), that personal identity is traced. The person who lives at 9 a.m. this morning is a result of the person who lived at 7 a.m. this morning.

Doctrine of Karma

It is in this sense that the Buddhist doctrine of karma has to be interpreted. Though some assume that the doctrine of karma is a metaphysical doctrine, it is actually a psychological principle or a law based on the law of causation as applied to a series of mental events. If a person has a 'bad' thought now, this will generate further 'bad' thoughts, thus gradually leading to the formation of a karmic mental complex. This complex can generate various types of mental illnesses like anxiety and guilt, which gradually lead to further complications such as physical illnesses. The Buddha said that karma is a principle that can be verified in this life itself by looking into the causal relationships between mental phenomena and between mental and physical phenomena. A 'bad' thought leads to tension and anxiety, while a 'good' thought leads to calmness and relaxation. Thus, the problem of personal identity and moral responsibility is solved in terms of causal connectedness.

Another problem that arises within Buddhist ethics is how to justify altruistic or 'other-regarding' action. If real 'persons' do not exist, how can we make the idea of moral commitment to others meaningful? A difficult problem that comes up in the Buddhist teaching of egolessness is 'why should I do anything at all'?

Before we discuss acting or working for others, we must first be clear about what is meant by 'work'. Ordinarily, work is supposed to be physical. But Buddhism accepts two kinds of work: physical and spiritual. For example, a Brahmin farmer called Kasībhāradvāja accused the Buddha of leading an idle life, not doing any physical work or labor. The Buddha replied that he was also engaged in labor and that he was perhaps engaged in a task more important and arduous than what physical labor involves. Further, he said that if necessary, his work could also be easily described in the jargon of the physical labor of a farmer. The Buddha answers, "I also, O Brahmana, both plough and sow, and having ploughed and sown, I eat." Then the Brahmin retorts: "Thou professest to be a ploughman, and yet we do not see thy ploughing; asked about thy ploughing, tell us of it, that we may know thy ploughing." The Buddha answers, "Faith is the seed, penance the rain, understanding my yoke and plough, modesty the pole of the plough, mind the tie, thoughtfulness my ploughshare and goad... Exertion is my beast of burden; carrying me to *Nibbāna,* he goes without turning back to the place where, having gone, one does not grieve. So this ploughing is ploughed, it bears the fruit of immortality; having ploughed this ploughing, one is freed from all pain."[1] Therefore, the Buddhist approach to asceticism should be properly understood. The Buddha recommended forests and lonely places only as ideal sites for training in meditation, but never for living, and he always advised monks that they "should travel around for the benefit and happiness of the multitude of human beings" (*Caratha bhikkhave cārikaṃ bahu jana hitāya bahujana sukhāya*).

Conventional Reality and Absolute Reality

Buddhism also formulates another distinction we should be aware of, that between two levels of reality: conventional reality and absolute reality. Persons and morality exist in the conventional realm, while in the realm of absolute reality both these ideas do not make much sense. Ordinary moral theory presupposes the sense of 'a person'. Ordinary moral theory is valid and meaningful for one who believes that he is 'a person'. Once one realizes that there is no person, then he goes beyond this type of morality. However, it should be clearly noted that by going beyond morality one does not get permission to contravene ordinary moral values. In other words, the absolute dimension has no power or privilege to abrogate ordinary moral values. The Buddha shows this distinction by saying that an ordinary person, when he is moral, is conditioned by morality (*sīlamayo*), but an enlightened person is moral by "nature" (*sīlavā*)[2], because the nature of Nirvana is moral perfection, *i.e.*, when viewed from the conventional standpoint. Therefore, when we discuss morality we must be aware of the conventional level of reality which is presupposed in our analysis.

"Other Regarding" Actions

How does Buddhism recommend and justify 'other-regarding' actions? It has several grounds for doing so. One reason stems from the theory of dependent origination (*paṭicca-samuppāda*), which emphasizes that everything originates dependent on everything else. Therefore, everything owes its existence to everything else. Actually, it is the *Anatta* doctrine that involves one in altruistic actions. The doctrine of interdependence rules out the possibility of a separate soul, because nothing can be independent in a world where everything is interrelated. I cannot think of myself as separate from the rest of the universe because, for example, if I take my body, it is dependent on food (which means that my body is dependent on plants, animals, water, oxygen, *etc.*). My mind also exists dependently because the existence of thoughts is dependent on sense data derived from the external world of objects and persons.

A Buddha's altruistic commitment to others and other objects originates from this dependency. Because my existence is dependent on the rest of the universe, I naturally owe a debt and an obligation to the rest of the universe. Therefore, my attitude to others and other objects should be one of respect and gratitude. Thus, Buddhism advocates a sense of awe and respect towards living beings and nature. Here, it is important to note that in Buddhism, the distinction between altruism and egoism breaks down as a meaningless distinction. The ideal moral attitude to other beings advocated by the

Buddha is the "love a mother shows towards her one and only child" and the love relationship between mother and child cannot be characterized as egoistic or altruistic because it is a fluid mixture of both. Likewise, helping others is a way of helping oneself.

One has to understand that one is a part of a larger whole, and is not a separate person. That is why the ordinary unenlightened man is, in Buddhist terminology, called a '*Puthujjana*' (*puthu* = separate; *jana* = people), or a person who believes that he is separate. The relationship between the part and whole is organic. In the way the whole creates the part, the part also creates the whole. Therefore one should realize that one can play a creative (in a cosmic sense) part in the cosmic order of events. In a way, the whole determines the part. But, the Buddhist point is that the part can also play a role in determining the whole. This is, of course, an inevitable implication of the principle of interrelatedness. Here, one can see that the Buddhist position highlights the nature of the problem of free will and determinism. One of the main teachings of the early Mahayana *Sutras* is that the nature of the ultimate reality is its paradoxicality. Free will being a part of the ultimate reality (as Kant also maintained), it may be that the principle of free will has to be inevitably understood as a paradoxical principle.

Hua-Yen Doctrine of Interdependence

The full implication of the Buddhist doctrine of interdependency were best explained by the Mahayana Buddhist school of thought called Hua-yen. Commenting on the Hua-yen doctrine Francis Cook says, "Existence therefore is neither absolutely existent, nor is it non-existent; it is contingently existent, and it is because of contingent or dependent being that progress in the Dharma is possible."

Referring to the Hua-yen argument that the building is dependent on the rafter and vice versa, Cook says, "Here, for the most part, Fa-tsang is concerned with arguing that the particular individual possesses total power to create the whole. The argument seems to be simple enough; if the rafter does not have this total power, then if the rafter is removed, the whole building should remain, just as my whole body should remain if a leg is amputated. Obviously this is not the case, and so Fa- tsang says that in order for the whole to be a whole, the part must exert total power in the formation of the whole. To possess total power means, as was said above, the causative power of the whole building. Partial power, on the other hand, is simply the power in the rafter itself. What this really means, presumably, is that if the rafter were to exert only the causative power of itself—*i.e.*, to exert the power of its rafterness—then it could never truly become integrated into the whole building, the rafter assumes the causative power of the whole building and thus acts as total cause for it. This is, in fact, nothing more than the kind of true interdependence which Hua-yen teaches."[3]

Cook quotes the Hua-yen Treatise: "Therefore you should know that the perfect building is inherent in the one rafter. Since it is inherent in this one rafter, you should know therefore that the rafter is the building. Question: since the building is identical with the rafter, then the remaining planks, tiles and so on, must be identical with the rafter aren't they? Answer: generally speaking, they are all identical with the rafter. The reason is that if you take away a rafter, there is no building, because if there is no rafter, the building is spoiled. And when you have a spoiled building, you cannot speak of planks, tiles and so on. Therefore, the planks, tiles, and so on, are identical with the rafter. If they are not the rafter, then the building is not formed, for planks, tiles, and so on, do not become formed either. Now, since they all are formed together, you should know that they are identical [with the rafter] Since this is so of the one rafter, the other rafters are the same. Therefore, if all the *dharmas* which constitute interdependent origination are not formed [as an integrated totality of interdependence], then they cease. If they are all formed [together], then they are all identical with each other, interfused, completely free in their interrelationships, extremely difficult to conceive, and surpass commonsense notions. The nature of things, which is interdependent origination, is universal, so you can understand everything else by analogy with the above example."[4]

Cook comments on this passage: "In this passage, which speaks of taking a rafter away from the building, there is some possibility of misreading Fa-tsang's intention. As has been mentioned several times, there is really no question of removing the part from the whole, at least if the whole is the whole of existence. Whether the whole be the greatest of wholes, or the body of a mouse, when a part is removed, the previously perfect whole is destroyed, it just is not that particular whole any more. The perfect whole is implied in the part in the sense that the whole becomes the whole only when the part is integrated into it and becomes the whole. If a part is removed, the previous whole now becomes a new whole and still the question of the relationship of the existent parts remains, because Hua-yen is concerned only with the question of the relationship pertaining among entities. Actually, even the disappearance of an entity acts as a condition for the whole and thus changes the configuration of the whole in some way, as noted by John Donne who said that 'any man's death diminishes me, because I am involved in mankind.' Death, disappearance, diminution: all these are events also, and constitute those conditions by which I *am* and by which I am defined. Moreover, the new appearance of an entity acts as a condition in the same way, not only affecting the present and future, but even the past, in the same way, according to T. S. Eliot, that a new poem retrospectively changes the whole history of literature as far back as the creation of the first poem.

"The last part of the preceding paragraph from the Treatise may be obscure partly because it is so terse and elliptical. However, if we keep in mind that the identity of the parts is due to their emptiness, and this emptiness is none other than the interdependence of these parts, much of the diffiuclty will be removed. The argument, paraphrased, is this: if the rafter is not integrated into the whole building, then we cannot speak of tiles, nails and the like, since they derive their existence from the existence of the rafter. The assemblage of particulars which is called 'building' and the one particular called 'rafter' thus act as necessary conditions for the existence at all in this interdependence, and it is this universal lack of self-existence which constitutes their identity. Thus, as Fa-tsang says, 'if all the dharmas which constitute interdependent origination are not formed [as an integrated totality of interdependence], then they cease'."[5]

What the doctrine of interdependence emphasizes is, from the fact that the rest of the universe is responsible for me, it follows that I too am responsible for the rest of the universe. In the *Sigālovāda Sutta,* the Buddha emphasizes that rights and duties imply each other.

If the rights are not well reciprocated by the duties, a moral imbalance is bound to result. From the fact that nature treats us rightly, it follows that we should treat nature rightly. Buddhism strongly believes that morality is the best way to communicate with nature because morality is the nature of nature. If we mishandle or mistreat nature we are bound to get back our due.

Love That Embraces All Beings

It is from the above considerations that an attitude of deepest love towards other beings and nature, which the Buddha advocates is derived. It is important to note that Buddhism is much more than merely humanistic, because the Buddhist love embraces all types of beings. Whenever the Buddha talks about loving others, he always speaks of 'all beings' (*sabbe sattā*). The same love that prompts a mother to care for her one and only son should prompt persons to do their best to help the rest of the community. This attitude fosters virtues like sharing and sympathy.

Another reason why we should do anything at all is grounded on sympathy. A central theme in Buddhist ethics is that 'one should treat others in exactly the same way as one treats oneself' (*attānaṃ upamaṃ katvā*). In the *Anumāna Sutta*, the Buddha states that the basis of the 'other-regarding' principle is an inference from oneself to another. The inference works in two ways. The first is thinking of oneself in terms of others. According to the Buddha, the sense of the value of oneself or of one's own personality is derived from others. Therefore, 'personality' itself being a value concept, if one is to become a 'person' in the proper sense, it must necessarily be done in a social medium. For that reason, one should always be considerate of the value of others. Man's personality is largely a product and an item of the society around him. One becomes good or derives any value to one's personality only through the society, which is why one must consider and respect others. One does not become oneself without the help of others. Here, the so-called distinction between altruism and egoism breaks down. The Buddha states his inferential principle: "Therein, your reverences, self ought to be measured against self thus by a monk: 'That person who is of evil desires and who is in the thrall of evil desires, that person is displeasing and disagreeable to me; and similarly, if I were of evil desires and in the thrall of evil desires, I would be displeasing and disagreeable to other'."[6] The dichotomy between egoism and altruism breaks down when he repeatedly emphasizes the necessity of 'other-regarding' virtues for one's development as a person, not only on a social level, but even on the spiritual level where progress is impossible without cultivating 'other-regarding' virtues.

Referring to a prerequisite for meditation it is stated, "He dwells, having suffused the first quarter with a mind of friendliness, likewise the second, likewise the third, likewise the fourth; just so above, below, across; he dwells having suffused the whole world everywhere, in everyway, with a mind of friendliness that is far-reaching, widespread, immeasurable, without enmity, without malevolence. He dwells having suffused the first quarter with a mind of compassion . . . sympathetic joy . . . equinimity . . . that is far-reaching, widespread, immeasurable, without enmity, without malevolence."[7] The Buddha preached that one's attitude towards other living beings should be similar to a mother's attitude towards her one and only son: "Just as a mother looks after her one and only son as her own life, one should look after all the living beings with an unlimited compassion."[8] A mother's love for her child is neither egoistic nor altruistic.

The second way of inference is considering others in terms of oneself. "For a state that is not pleasant or delightful to me must be so to him also; and a state that is not pleasing or delightful to me: how could I inflict that upon another? As a result of such reflection, he himself abstains from taking the life of any creature and he encourages others so to abstain, and speaks in praise of so abstaining. Thus, as regards bodily conduct, he is utterly pure."[9] (The Buddha goes on to elaborate that one should think similarly with regard to other moral principles also). Here he is suggesting the intrinsic value of other persons, in the only way that is possible to do it, through empathy or sympathetic feelings. It is an ultimate moral justification. Kant approximates the Buddhist ideal when he talks about the treatment of other persons as ends in themselves. But the Buddha goes much further when he advocates the treatment of all beings as ends in themselves. The Buddha maintains that life is the only ultimate, intrinsic and sacred value in this universe.

In the *Karaṇīya Metta Sutta* he says that, in spreading love, one must think of all possible types of beings: "Whatever living beings there may be: feeble or strong, long (or tall), stout, or medium, short, small, or large, seen or unseen, those dwelling far or near, those who are born and those who are yet to be born: may all beings, without exception, be happy-minded."[10] We must respect all forms of life. What the Buddha believes is that whatever form it takes, life is life. As the Mahayanists say, all life forms are sacred because they all contain the seeds of Buddhahood or perfection. If one does not have this reverence towards life, one alienates oneself from life. Whether it is one's own or another's, life is treated as a commonly shared property. If one disrespects life that is manifested in any form, one deteriorates morally and spiritually because one becomes alienated from the most basic and intrinsic value of the world. Here, it is important to note the significant fact that the Buddha prohibited monks from harming trees and plants because "they are creatures with one sense-faculty (*ekindriya*), (*i.e.* touch)" and therefore, "people are of the opinion that there is life in trees."[11] He also forbade monks to dig the earth because that would harm "tiny creatures living in earth"[12] (But he did not enjoin these rules for laymen because of the practical difficulties).

Although a complete practice of *Ahiṃsā* (non-injury) is even theoretically impossible because the process of living itself automatically involves a process of killing or injuring many beings, perfect *Ahiṃsā* is always regarded as the ideal that one should always try to live up to as far as possible. What truly matters is this genuine desire or motive to respect life. The Buddha says that the ultimate and intrinsic value of slife will be self evident to any one who will care to look at one's own life. The Buddha's appeal to us is to realize that all other beings also think of themselves exactly in the same way one thinks about oneself. Therefore, in Buddhism, the sacredness of life is an ultimate ethical fact which is proved and made meaningful self- evidently, *i.e.*, through empathy.

Morality and Salvific Power

Another important ground for moral commitment is the fact

that morality has salvific power and potency. The four cardinal virtues of Buddhism are love, compassion, sympathetic joy and neutrality. The cultivation of these virtues, when coupled with wisdom, gradually leads one to Nirvana. The Buddha emphasizes that morality and wisdom are interrelated and interactive: "From morality comes wisdom and from wisdom morality . . . Like washing one hand with another . . . so is morality washed round with wisdom and wisdom with morality."[13] In the Buddhist tradition it is often said that since the attainment of insight is a comparatively difficult process, one should initially start with the practice of morality. Also, the establishment of oneself in morality is regarded as a kind of necessary prerequisite for the practice of insight. Buddhaghosa emphasizes this point when he quotes the famous verse: "After having established onself in morality, one should train mind and wisdom" (*Sīle patiṭṭhāya naro sapañño, cittaṃ paññaṃ ca bhāvayaṃ*). Practicing morality is easier than the intellectual exercise of wisdom. The practice of morality leads one towards the understanding of the true nature of things. For example, the practice of *Dāna* (or charity) leads to empathy, the development of which leads one to the identification of oneself with others. What happens at that point is, one experiences the noble truth of *Anatta* or Soullessness with regard to oneself. On the other hand, a correct vision of reality as *Anatta* and interdependence prompts one to share with, give and be kind to others.

Thus, the Buddha once explained how the practice of morality gradually leads to the ultimate salvation: "So you see, Ananda, good conduct has freedom from remorse as object and profit; freedom from remorse has joy; joy has rapture; rapture has calm; calm has happiness; happiness has concentration; concentration has seeing things as they really are; seeing things as they really are has revulsion and fading of interest; revulsion and fading of interest have release by knowing and seeing as their object and profit. So you see, Ananda, good conduct gradually leads to the summit."[14]

The Theory of Rebirth Supports Social Virtues

Another reason for moral and social commitment originates from the Buddhist theory of rebirth. According to this theory, we have been cycling in Samsara for a immeasurable period and during this period we have been relating ourselves to an infinite number of beings. Therefore, most of the beings that live in this cosmos have been, in one time or another, our close relatives, fathers or mothers, or close friends. Thus, this hypothesis or belief should be always in the back of our minds and prompt us to practice social virtues because this belief imposes a kind of moral obligation to reach out and help others.

In Buddhism, altruistic actions assume such a significant place that the ethics of the later school of Buddhism, Mahayana, devoted its dominant and exclusive emphasis on this when it developed the doctrine of the Bodhisattva. However, it should not be forgotten that the Bodhisattva ideal is equally central to early Buddhism, as it is emphasized in the *Jātakas* or the stories of the former lives of the Buddha. These *Jātaka* tales play a very active and important role in the minds of the Buddhists. Mahayana developed this concept in great detail to its logical extreme. A Bodhisattva is a person who postpones his ultimate attainment of Nirvana for the sake of all other beings. One becomes a Bodhisattva by taking the vow that he will not pass into Nirvana until he has helped the last blade of grass to attain Nirvana. Thus he vows to devote his whole life for the benefit of all sentient beings. Therefore, the Bodhisattva concept portrays the ultimate stage of perfect altruism. Thus, from the point of view of the Bodhisattva ideal, the question would be, not "Why should I do anything at all?", but, "Why am I not doing everything possible to help others?"

3

Criteria of Good and Bad

The *summum bonum* of Buddhist morality is Nirvana. Therefore, the attainment of Nirvana becomes the ultimate criterion of good. Nirvana signifies the absence of the three basic Samsaric evils: greed or liking (*lobha*), hatred or disliking (*dosa*) and ignorance (*moha*). The Buddha has treated the actions of liking and disliking as similar to each other because disliking is only a negative form of liking. In order to attain Nirvana, one has to discard not only likes but dislikes as well. Therefore, the three characteristics of Nirvana are: the absence of greed (*alobha*), the absence of hatred (*adosa*) and the absence of ignorance (*amoha*). Any action, physical, vocal or mental, that leads towards these three characteristics is termed good, while any action that opposes these three is termed bad.

Here we should clarify the Buddhist concepts normally translated as 'good' and 'bad'. Although *Akusala* and *Pāpa* are translated as 'bad', and *Kusala* and *Puñña* as 'good', and are also often used as synonymous pairs in the Buddhist texts, there are very important, subtle differences to be noted among these concepts. The term *Pāpa* is common to Hinduism as well and refers to evil, and in Buddhism it is often personified as *Māra*, one of whose epithets is *Pāpimant* or 'the Evil One'. The specific Buddhist word used for good is *Kusala* which means 'efficient' or 'capable', that is, what is good is what is efficient in (or capable of) leading towards Nirvana. *Akusala* is its opposite. *Puñña* is a term common also to Hinduism and means merit, and an action that generates *Puñña* is called a *Puñña Kamma*. Here, the emphasis is on making merit. Merit-making actions have been treated by the Buddha as inferior kinds of moral actions because accumulation of merits can hinder one's spiritual salvation by leading one to births that involve long periods of existence, like those of the *Devas* and *Brahmas*. Therefore, in a sense, a *Puñña Kamma* could be an *Akusala Kamma*. *Kusala* and *Akusala Kammas* are performed only by persons who have entered into the spiritual path. When an ignorant person kills an animal, he is doing a *Pāpa Kamma*, not an *Akusala Kamma*, and is consequently accruing *Pāpa*. If someone practices charity with a wish to be born in heaven, he is accumulating *Puñña*. One cannot accumulate *Kusala*, rather it makes one capable of realizing Nirvana. The Buddha defines *Kusala* (or 'good') as follows: "There are three roots of good. What are the three? Absence of greed, absence of hatred and absence of delusion. Whatever the non-greedy one performs with body, speech and thought, that is good. What the non-greedy one, not overwhelmed by greed, whose mind is controlled, does not do to another by unjustly causing him suffering through punishment, loss of wealth, abuse, banishment, on the grounds that 'might is right'—that also is good. Thus, these good conditions born of non-greed, conjoined with non-greed, arising from non-greed, resulting from non-greed are assembled together in him."[1] Thus, in Buddhist morality, the end can, and does, justify the means because the end is spiritual salvation.

What this analysis shows is that Buddhism does not regard 'goodness' as a moral absolute. In contemporary terminology, Buddhism propounds a prescriptive theory of ethics. A Buddhist ethical proposition can be divided into two parts: a factual component and a value component. The factual component is extremely important because the Buddha strongly believed that 'ought' did not imply 'can'. In other words, we must not say we 'ought' to do something unless it is something that we 'can' do. Therefore, 'ought' should be based on reality or facts. This is why the factual component becomes important. The value component should be based on the factual component. The meaning and validity of the value component depends on the truth of the factual component. If the factual component is false, then the value component becomes meaningless and invalid. For example, if one makes the value judgment that 'killing animals is good' we must see whether it is grounded in true facts. Thus, when we look at its factual component, we see that its factual component is false because animals 'do not like death'. Therefore, the Buddha emphasizes this important relationship between 'value' and 'fact'. This was partly because of his central thesis that any judgment, value or otherwise, should be based on a theory of facts as they are (*yathābhūta*). In that sense, the theory of reality logically precedes the theory of morality. If we take the first Buddhist precept that 'killing is bad', the Buddha has justified this proposition by clarifying the two components involved: "Taking oneself as an example, one should not harm or kill others" (*Attānaṃ upamaṃ katvā na haneyya na ghātaye*)—the value component. This value judgment is based on the fact that "All beings dislike punishment or harming, and all are afraid of death" (*Sabbe tasanti daṇḍassa, sabbe bhāyanti maccuno*)[2]—the factual component. When the Buddha speaks of specific ethical rules or regulations, he makes the prescriptive component more explicit. One of the rules he formulated for monks was that they should not eat any solid food after midday until the following morning. This was made meaningful in regard to the end in view, namely that it will be conducive to a light physique which facilitate a good medium for meditation, the immediate aim of monkhood. But the Buddha also said that if one cannot have a light and a comfortable physique due to some form of illness, etc., then even after midday one should take a nutritious and concentrated light food like ghee (rarified butter). Conforming to the mere letter of the precepts without having the mind focused on the ultimate goal, was criticized as "clinging to precepts and vows" (*sīlabbata parāmāsa*). In this way, all Buddhist ethical rules gain their value and validity in terms of the ultimate spiritual ideal. Every ethical rule is a prescription to achieve or approximate that ideal. It is significant that the Buddha is often reffered to in Buddhist literature, as a 'physician'.

Therefore, the Buddhist theory of ethics maintains that morality has a hypothetical nature, because if the reality or the circumstances were to change, the ethical values would necessarily change too. This shows that Buddhist ethics is utilitarian. It is an ideal utilitarianism rather than a hedonistic one because the ultimate end of the ethical endeavor goes beyond the pleasure-pain principle. Also, what is emphasized is the utility of the act, rather than the utility of the rule. In performing an act, the whole context of the act—motive, means and the act itself—has to be taken into consideration.

This raises the issue whether Buddhist ethics is teleological or deontological: teleology is performing an action with the expectation of results for oneself; deontology means performing an action merely for the sake of doing it. Kant was the major exponent of deontology in the West. Deontological actions are treated as superior because they tend to deemphasize oneself and emphasize others. Buddhist Ethics contains both these aspects, while at some stage it transcends this dichotomy as well. Buddhist morality operates on three levels or spheres: (1) karmic level, (2) path level, and (3) enlightened level. The karmic level is samsaric or worldly. By doing good actions with a wish for samsaric results, one can reap good fruits. If you give in charity, it is a way of getting more later in this life or in a life to come. The Buddha says that he preached the benefits of karmic actions partly to state a moral truth and partly to attract people to spiritual life by tempting them through this type of 'worldly' motivation. Thus he used it as an *upāya* or a skillful means when he said, for example, that "charity is a ladder to heaven" (*Dānaṃ saggassa sopānaṃ*). But the karmic actions are morally inferior because they are based on the principle of greed or liking. By karmic actions all one does is lengthen one's life span in samsara since one will be reborn in long-lasting life-forms as one becomes bound by the inexorable law of karma to reap the full fruits of one's karmic actions. It is through karmic actions that one accumulates *Puñña* and *Pāpa*. *Puñña-karmic* actions are clearly teleological. Although the Buddha recommended karmic actions for their initial attractiveness and for the preliminary training it gives in morality, he emphasized that it was a self-oriented and inferior mode of ethical action and should therefore be transcended by path action. He says: "Monks, [if] a monk fares the religious life aspiring after some class of gods, thinking: 'By this moral habit or custom or austerity or religious life I will become a god or one among gods', his mind does not incline to ardor, to continual application, to perseverance, to striving."[3]

Path action is disinterested action. One is only interested in the act, never in the fruit. But there is a slight teleology involved here because the path action is performed for a particular purpose, namely, to achieve disinterestedness which leads to enlightenment. Although this subtle teleological element is present, the nature of this teleology is highly paradoxical because the ideal of enlightenment is a form of disinterestedness. The nature of this paradoxicality should be clearly noted here. However, in performing a path action the motive should be clearly deontological. Here, it is interesting to speculate whether there can ever be completely deontological actions, because a subtle teleology is necessarily presupposed in any deontological action, in the sense that one performs deontological imperatives because one needs to perfect oneself, and here one has ethical perfection as the goal.

Karmic Actions and Path Actions

An action can be performed as a karmic action or as a path action, the difference being only a matter of perspective. If one gives charity wishing for samsaric fruits, it becomes a karmic action. When one practices charity on the path level, one not only does not wish for any results but one does not relate one's mind to any object or any thing, because one's mind is to be established on the true nature of things. When performed from the path perspective, one gives charity realizing that there is no giver, no gift, no receiver, because none of these really exist for a person at this level of understanding.

The nature of this deontology is best explained in the celebrated Mahayana text, *Vajracchedikā Prajñāpāramitā*, where the Buddha says, "Moreoever, Subhuti, a Bodhisattva who gives a gift should not be supported by a thing, nor should he be supported anywhere. When he gives gifts he should not be supported by sight-objects, not by sounds, smells, tastes, touchables, or mind-objects. For, Subhuti, the Bodhisattva, the great being, should give gifts in such a way that he is not supported by the notion of a sign."[4] He cannot think, for example, that there is a receiver of the gift because all beings are ultimately no beings and, "if in a Bodhisattva the notion of a 'being' should take place, he could not be called a '*Bodhi*-being'. And why? He is not to be called a Bodhi-being, in whom the notion of a self or of a being should take place, or the notion of a living soul or of a person."[5]

In this path level itself, one can see some tendencies going beyond the deontological level, because, besides the deontological doctrine, it also has a separate doctrine about the nature of reality. This is best seen when the Sutra states, "Therefore then, Subhuti, the *Bodhi*-being, the great being, after he has got rid of all perceptions, should raise his thought to the utmost, right and perfect enlightenment. He should produce a thought which is unsupported by forms, sounds, smells, tastes, touchables, or mind-objects, unsupported by dharma, unsupported by no-dharma, unsupported by anything. And why? All supports have actually no support. It is for this reason that the *Tathāgata* teaches: By an unsupported Bodhisattva should a gift be given, not by one who is supported by forms, sounds, smells, tastes, touchables, or mind-objects."[6]

The tendency of the Bodhisattva's actions to go beyond the realm of deontology is further clarified in the *Pañcaviṃsatisāhasrikā*:

"Sariputra: 'What is the worldly, and what is the supramundane perfection of giving?'

"Subhuti: 'The worldly perfection of giving consists in this: The Bodhisattva gives liberally to all those who ask, all the while thinking in terms of real things. It occurs to him: 'I give, that one receives, this is the gift. I renounce all my possessions without stint. I act as one who knows the Buddha. I practice the perfection of giving. I, having made this gift into the common property of all beings, dedicate it to supreme enlightenment, and that without apprehending anything. By means of this gift and its fruit may all beings in this very life be at their ease, and may they one day enter Nirvana!' Tied by three ties, he gives a gift. Which three? A perception of self, a perception of others, a perception of the gift. "The supramundane perfection of giving, on the other hand, consists in the threefold purity. What is the three-fold purity? Here a Bodhisattva gives a gift, and he does not apprehend a self, nor a recipient, nor a gift; also no reward of his giving. He surrenders that gift to all beings, but he apprehends neither beings nor self. He dedicates that gift to supreme enlightenment, but he does not apprehend any enlightenment. This is called the supramundane perfection of giving."[7]

This passage distinguishes between two stages of Bodhisattva actions. In the first stage, the worldly actions he does are clearly deontological because they are done for the sake of others. There is self-oriented teleology, which is, of course, implicitly presupposed in all deontological actions.

In the second, or the supramundane stage, the Bodhisattva's actions enter into a completely different, higher dimension. In any deontological giving, three things are presupposed: a self, a receiver and a gift. Here the Bodhisattva is asked not only to go beyond these three conceptions, but also not to hold the idea of moral perfection or enlightenment. Therefore, the second stage is a movement beyond the deontological dimension, too. For while path action starts with a deontological dimension, it ends with a transcendence of that dimension. Thus, the last stages of Buddhist ethics cannot be categorized by available analytical categories.

Does this mean that no merits accrue in performing path actions? Actually, when one is not interested in merits as a path-actor, it is said that the merits one accrues are so vast that they are incalculable. "... the heap of merit of that *Bodhi*-being, who unsupported gives a gift, is not easy to measure. What do you think, Suhuti, is the extent of space in the East easy to measure?—Subhuti replied: 'No indeed, O Lord'—... Even so the heap of merit of that *Bodhi*-being who unsupported gives a gift is not easy to measure."[8] But the irony is that by the time he starts accumulating these huge heaps of merit, he has come to realize the true nature of merits as well, namely that they are 'no heaps' of merit. Subhuti explains that "the *Tathāgata* spoke of the 'heap of merit' as a non-heap."[9]

If we call the Bodhisattva's actions deontological, then how are we going to characterize a Buddha's actions? In the case of the Buddha, the Bodhisattva's deontological motive is conspicuously absent.

A realized person is said to have gone beyond morality. In the *Sutta Nipāta*, the Buddha describes the saint as one who has gone beyond good and bad. "... the noble man who does not cling to what has been seen, or heard, to virtue and (holy) works, or to what has been thought, to what is good and to what is bad, and who leaves behind what has been grasped, without doing anything in this world, he does not acknowledge that purification comes from another."[10] Elsewhere, this idea is again emphasized "By good deeds one goes to heaven, by bad deeds to unhappy abodes. By the destruction of (good and bad) deeds one attains cessation with a liberated mind, like the flame with the cessation of fuel."[11] Once the Buddha, speaking of Sariputta, says, "He has attained to mastery, he has attained to going beyond in the noble moral habit, he has attained to mastery . . . "[12] Here it should be clearly emphasized that by going beyond morality, the saint is not in a privileged position to abrogate ordinary morality.

This distinction between the religious dimension and the moral dimension is very clear in theistic religions, and it is this distinction that has sometimes led to the justification of the killing of human beings in the name of religion. As evident from the time of the *Bhagavadgītā*, when the killing of even one's close relatives was justified in the name of religion, to the present day, this justification of the holy war has led to disastrous results in the killing of countless numbers of people. Therefore, this kind of justification is a dangerous loop-hole to be left open in the religious dimension.

In Budhism there is no possibility of this happening, since Buddhism has never waged holy wars. There are two reasons for this. One is, according to Buddhism, there is a causal or a generic relationship between morality and salvation. The other is that ultimate reality is by nature moral. In other words, the religious dimension does not differ from the moral dimension in a qualitative sense. The religious dimension is really a furthering or a heightening or a completion of the moral dimension. The Buddhist saint becomes moral by nature. Therefore, Buddhism preaches that ultimate reality is moral even by the standards of ordinary conventional morality. The difference between an ordinary moral person and a saint is that "the saint is moral by nature while the ordinary person is conditioned by morality" (*sīlavā hoti no ca sīlamayo*).[13] When a saint performs an action, only the action is there (*kiriyamatta*).[14] It is more a happening than an action, because there is no motive in the sense that 'he' 'has' neither a teleological end in view nor a motive to conform to any categorical imperative.

Can one say that a realized person's actions are deontological?

They are not even deontological because the saint goes beyond the sphere of deontology. A Buddha need not and does not practice charity. Charity is his very nature. His acts can be characterized only as spontaneous happenings. It is here we see how Buddhist ethics transcends the dichotomy between telelogy and deontology.

Objective Justification of Moral Actions

In Buddhism moral justifications are made on several grounds. We saw above that 1) empathy, 2) the salvific power of morality, and 3) the nature of reality are three basic grounds for such justifications. Of these, empathy offers a way to justify moral actions in Buddhism without reference to specifically 'religious' concepts. The Buddha taught that there were still more ways in which this might be done.

The Buddha always found the justification of moral values in the consequences they generically produce. He condemned bad actions on three grounds (1) the self upbraids the self; (2) society condemns the evildoer; (3) the evildoer will be reborn in a bad form of existence. Here one might think that, to a certain extent, Buddhism requires its religious context to make its morality meaningful because another person who does not believe in rebirth might not be able to make full sense out of Buddhist morality. In fact, the Buddha pointedly answered this question when he formulated his moral wager: If one believes in effective (*i.e.*, moral) action (as involving rebirth), then one will be praised here and also be born in good conditions. So one has victory in two ways. If one does not believe in effective action, one loses in both ways.[15] He elaborates this elsewhere. " 'If I do good, if there be a world beyond, if there be ripening of fruit and ripening of deeds done well or ill, then, when the body breaks up after death, I shall be reborn in the Happy Lot, in the heavenly world . . . If, however, there be no world beyond, no fruit and ripening of deeds done well or ill, yet in this very life do I hold myself free from enmity and oppression, sorrowless and well.' "[16] What the Buddha is trying to show is that Buddhist ethics and moral values can be meaningful even outside the religious context of Buddhism. Therefore, here, morality logically precedes religion in two ways. One, the Buddha accepted that morality does make perfect sense even outside the strictly religious context. The other is that moral values are values that society in general and men in particular do actually follow. To be moral is to be a happy person as an individual. The Buddha states, "It is the guilty dread, housefather, which he who kills begets in this very life, as a result of his killing it is that guilty dread about the future life, which he who kills begets: that feeling of painful dejection felt by him, that guilty dread, is allayed in him who abstains from killing."[17] Therefore, "He, possessed of the Noble body of moral habit, subjectively experiences unsullied well-being."[18]

Individual and Social Morality

As we kept emphasizing before, the distinction between individual morality and social morality becomes blurred from the Buddhist perspective. Buddhaghosa comments: "Furthermore, on account of his unvirtuousness an unvirtuous person is displeasing to deities and human beings, is uninstructable by his fellows in the life of purity, suffers when unvirtuousness is censured, and is remorseful when the virtuous are praised. Owing to that unvirtuousness he is as ugly as hemp cloth. Contact with him is painful because those who fall in with his views are brought to long-lasting suffering, the states of loss. He is worthless because he causes no great fruit (to accrue) to those who give him gifts. He is as hard to purify as a cesspit many years old. He is like a log from a pyre, . . . He is always nervous, like a man who is everyone's enemy. He is as unfit to live with as a dead carcass. Though he may have the qualities of learning, *etc.*, he is as unfit for the homage of his fellows in the life of purity as a charnel-ground fire is for that of brahmanas. He is as incapable of reaching the distinction of attainment as a blind man is of seeing a visible object."[19] Moral values get related to religion in the way that they are, as a matter of fact, causally conducive to attaining the spiritual goal.

In deciding a complicated moral issue, Buddhism advocates that one should consult three things, the first being one's conscience (*attādhipateyya*). Here, it is important to note that Buddhism regards conscience as sometimes fallible, and not a sufficient criterion in all situations. Therefore, it should be supplemented by two other moral guides. And so, secondly, one must consult 'the opinion of the world' (*lokādhipateyya*), and thirdly, one should consult the Dhamma (*dhammādhipateyya*).

4

Karma and Rebirth

Karma and rebirth have often been treated as metaphysical concepts. But a close look at them will show that in Buddhism they are used as experientially verifiable concepts. The major purport of the principle of karma is to explain that one makes oneself. One is the creator of oneself. The Buddha states this principle: one "is of one's own making, the heir to deeds (*kamma*), deeds are the matrix, deeds are the kin, deeds are the foundation; whatever one does, good or bad, one will become heir to that."[1] One's karma or one's deeds follow oneself. The *Dhammapada* starts with the following twin-verses: "All that we are is the result of what we have thought: we are founded on our thoughts, we are made up of our thoughts. If a man speaks or acts with an evil thought, pain follows him, as the wheel follows the foot of the ox that draws the carriage. All that we are is the result of what we have thought: we are founded on our thoughts, we are made up of our thoughts. If a man speaks or acts with a pure thought, happiness follows him, like a shadow that never leaves him." In other words, one is what one makes of oneself. Thus the principle of karma highlights the power of initiative and freedom a man possesses.

Free Will as Moral Choice

As K.N. Jayatilleke states, "the Buddha says that there is such a thing as 'an element of initiative' (*ārabbha-dhātu*) and as a result one can observe beings acting with initiative and this, says the Buddha, is what is called 'the free will of people' (*sattānaṃ atta-kāro*). He also goes on to say that there is 'an element of origination' (*nikkama-dhātu*), an 'element of endeavor' (*parakkama-dhātu*), an 'element of strength' (*thāma-dhātu*), an 'element of perseverance' (*ṭhiti-dhātu*) and an 'element of volitional effort' (*upakkama-dhātu*), which makes beings of their own accord act in various ways and that this showed that there was such a thing as free will."[2]

This free will manifests itself as moral choice. A person is free in the sense that he is able to choose alternative moral actions. One is free only in the realm of morality. As far as his physical realm is concerned he is determined by the web of interdependence. He may be able to influence this realm too, but it can be done only through the realm of morality. When one gets identified with morality (*sīlavā*) one becomes one with the ultimate reality; the secret lies here.

Karma and Motive

The Buddha defined karma as motive: "O Bhikkhus, I call the motive to be the deed" (*Cetanāhaṃ Bhikkhave kammaṃ vadāmi*).[3] This does not mean that the nature and effects of actions can be disregarded. In the Buddha's teachings, the word '*cetanā*' is a complex term that covers both that which is technically distinguished as 'intention' and 'motive', and the action as a consequence of the motive (or intention). With regard to actions that are bad though the end-motive is good, e.g., stealing money to give for charity, the Buddha would regard them as proceeding from two 'motives' and consequently as two actions. Though the motive is emphasized, the Buddha advises that one should critically examine the end action. For example, he says that when one gives charity, one should critically reflect or investigate whether the end action would have any bad side effects (*viceyya dānam dātabbaṃ*).

Thus, as karma has been defined as the motive, the law of karma should be interpreted essentially as a psychological law. Its basic tenet is that if one now produces a bad thought, as a result of that thought, more bad thoughts will arise, thus leading to a series of polluted, bad thoughts. These bad thoughts produce anxiety and tension and this resultant suffering is termed the fruit of bad karma. Likewise, good karma (i.e. good actions or deeds) will produce opposite results like happiness and calmness which are phenomena that we can easily verify in terms of our own experiences. Therefore, the Buddha regarded the law of karma as an experientially self-evident principle. The Buddhist theory of karma can be best explained in terms of C.G. Jung's theory of complexes. The Buddha teaches that there are two levels of mind: conscious and unconscious (*sampajañña mano saṃkhāra, asampajañña mano saṃkhāra*).[4] Although a bad thought may seem to disappear from the conscious mind, it does not completely disappear but goes down to the unconscious mind and settles there. When more bad thoughts arise that are related to the original bad thought, they all gradually go down to the unconscious and start forming a complex around the original nucleus. As bad thoughts are always emotionally charged, the complex becomes charged with more and more power as it grows bigger with more and more bad thoughts. This is called the maturation of karma (*kamma paripāka*). When the complex is fully matured, at some point it explodes into the fruition of the karma (*kamma vipāka*). A karma always attains fruition in a way that is similar to the original act performed and this is called the similarity between the act and the result (*kamma sarikkhatā*). A karma comes to maturation in order to bear fruit. There is a proper time for fruition. For example, if a person's good karma is dominant, the fruition of a bad karma will be postponed until a time when his good karma weakens. Therefore, the result of a karma may not be immediately evident because it may bear fruit in this life or in another life. Usually, the result of a karma is said to be several fold the impetus of the original action. The law of karma is inexorable, because it is the law of causation, and a karma cannot be annulled, or its effects avoided. However, the effects of a bad karma may be mitigated, to a certain extent, by performing a massive amount of good actions or good karma.

A good illustration of the working of the principle of karma is the story of the monk called Cakkhupala.[5] In a former life when he was a practicing eye surgeon, motivated by immoral intentions, he blinded the eyes of a patient. Consequently, in his current life his eyes went blind. Results of karma can assume many complicated forms. Immoral thought complexes could lead to neurotic and schizophrenic situations. The Buddha says that bad thoughts make one's blood unhealthy, manifesting in various organic illnesses. According to Buddhism, thoughts are infused with power, and one can 'do' good or bad things with thoughts. Bad thought complexes can attract one to evil situations or generate evil situations.

It should be clearly noted that the Buddha did not maintain that all that happens to a person is karmic. He called that belief "karmic determinism" and strongly criticized and rejected it. He held that if this theory were true then no room would exist for any moral discourse: "If one experiences happiness or misery solely as a result of past actions (*pubbekatahetu*), then one is only experiencing the results of past action and is, therefore, not responsible for his present actions."[6] According to the Buddha, the law of karma (*kamma niyama*) was only one of the laws of nature. If I feel hot now it is not due to the *Kammaniyāma* but due to the law of seasons (*utuniyāma*) because it is summer. Another such law is the law of seeds (*bīja niyāma*). For example, one's appearance is largely the result of one's genetic heritage. However, the Buddha did apply the law of karma to explain the widely differing states of existence: "Karma divides beings as superior or inferior" (*kammaṃ satte vibhajati yadidaṃ hīnappanī-tatāyāti*).

Karma and rebirth are intimately related. Karma is the fuel for rebirth. The destruction of karma ends (*kammakkhaya*) the process of rebirth. Beings can be reborn anywhere in the universe, but they are most often reborn among familiar relations and friends, due to karma. For example, if you owe me a big debt, there is a high probability that we might be reborn near each other.

The concept of rebirth is not specific to Buddhism. It is a widely dominant and a central idea in all Eastern religions. What makes the Buddhist idea of rebirth significantly different from the rest is that while all the other theories explain rebirth with the idea of a transmigrating soul, the Buddhists explain it with the idea of no soul. As explained above, the Buddhists account for personal identity in terms of unbroken causal continuity. However, there is an additional problem in rebirth. When we talk of a person's identity in this life, we have two criteria of identity: physical and mental. But in the case of rebirth the physical form changes and therefore we do not have the physical criterion of identity. But the continuity of mental events is there, and it is in terms of that continuity that we speak of the identity of two persons who have been living in two different births. The paradoxical nature of this identity is well stated when the *Milinda Pañha* says, referring to the person living now, that he is "neither the same person, nor a different person (*na ca so, na ca añño*)[7] from the one that lived in the previous birth." He is not the same person because the physical form is different, but he is not a different person either because mentally he is the same person due to the unbroken continuity of the series of mental events. Though he may be definitely changed mentally, that change is not a problem for identity, because, though our physical form changes radically from infancy to adulthood, we nevertheless maintain strict identity in terms of the continuity of the series of physical events.

Rebirth as a Probable Hypothesis

In Buddhism, rebirth is never meant to be accepted as a dogmatic article of faith. Until one verifies its truth, a Buddhist accepts it as a probable hypothesis to account for many unexplainable things like the highness and lowness of beings, the inborn gifted capacities of human beings, *etc.*, and this acceptance is based on a faith born of rational reflection (*ākāravatī saddhā*) and one is advised to go beyond this state of acceptance to the state of personal verification and become a person who has left faith behind (*assaddho*). The Buddha said that one could directly verify it through the extrasensory perceptual capacity called "the knowledge of previous births (*pubbenivāsānussati ñāṇa*) and said that anyone who wishes could acquire these extrasensory capacities by practicing meditational techniques.

When the Buddha spoke about rebirth to skeptical 'intellectuals' (*viññūpurisa*), he respected their skepticism and formulated the doctrine of rebirth as a wager. As explained above, the Buddha said, that if one believes in rebirth, one will win on two counts. If one does not believe in rebirth, and if rebirth happens to be true, then one will lose on two counts. Therefore, the Buddha's point was that a believer in rebirth will necessarily win, even if rebirth were false, while a disbeliever could lose, at least on one count. Another important phenomenological significance of the belief in rebirth is the powerful moral perspective it lends to altruistic activities, as we discussed above, by suggesting that other beings could have been closely related to oneself in previous births.

The other important consideration is that the truth or meaning of the fundamental message of Buddhism—the attainment of Nirvana—is not at all necessarily dependent on the truth of the idea of rebirth. Nirvana is a state of being beyond time and space and a state that may be attained 'right now'. However, if the idea of rebirth is not factually true, it would affect certain other doctrinal matters in Buddhism. For example, the whole of the *Jātaka* tradition is based on the concept of rebirth and Nirvana is also supposed to lead to the extinction of the process of rebirth (*bhavanirodho nibbānaṃ*).

What is the process of rebirth? This question was not discussed in detail in early Buddhism. It only mentions that for the birth of a human being, three things are necessary: father and mother should join, the mother should be in the fertile period, and a '*Gandhabba*' (the 'intermediate being' in the sense that the *Gandhabba* is in between two existences of births) should have arrived at the place ready for conception. The whole process of death and rebirth is most comprehensively discussed by the *Tibetan School of Buddhism* in the Tibetan Book of the Dead.[8] Soon after death the person assumes a subtle invisible form of material body and enters into an intermediate state of existence called the *Bardo* state, which lasts for a few days, depending on the strength of one's karma. One stays there floating around while looking for a fitting or a deserving rebirth, which is decided by one's karma, or the way one has conditioned or trained one's mind. As it is explained in the *Kukkuravatika Sutta*, if a person thinks and behaves like a dog or a god in this life, he will be accordingly attracted to the birth state of a dog or a god.[9]

Scientific Investigation of Rebirth

Recently, the hypothesis of rebirth has been subjected to scientific investigation by various researchers. Notable among them is Ian Stevenson, who first published his findings in "Twenty Cases Suggestive of Reincarnation".[10] He is primarily interested in one type of evidence for rebirth, namely, the cases of spontaneous memories. Stevenson has found some people in differing religio-cultural contexts having spontaneous memories about their previous births. After scientifically ruling out the possibility of gaining such knowledge in their present lives, he objectively verified their claims and found them true. An interesting fact is that some of these persons had certain fluent skills not learned in this life, which they claim to have learned and practiced in a previous life. In this way, rebirth is a useful and meaningful hypothesis to explain such things as the possession of various skills from birth. Another significant fact is that some claimants possessed birthmarks that were said to be related to incidents in a previous life. He documents a case in which a person's right hand was badly deformed because he had killed a person in a previous life with that hand.

Another source of evidence has come from research utilizing deep hypnosis. As we explained above, our past thoughts are stored in our unconscious; if one could probe a person's unconscious by deep hypnosis, one should be able to uncover memories of past births. In this way, by regressing a person through hypnosis, memories of previous lives have been unearthed.[11] An interesting fact found in this research was that when some persons were regressed into previous lives, they at once acquired the ability to speak fluently the languages that they spoke during that life while in the hypnotic trance.

Some investigations have been done into the experience of death, with the help of people who have had near-death experiences.[12] It is interesting to note that insofar as they go into the process of death, these recent findings significantly confirm the basic teachings of the *Tibetan Book of the Dead.*

5

Sublime Virtues

The most central moral virtues in Buddhism are love (*mettā*) compassion (*karuṇā*), sympathetic joy (*muditā*), and equanimity (*upekkhā*). These are called the four *Brahmavihāras* because Brahma is supposed to cultivate these virtues. When the Buddha preached to the Brahamins, he advocated the cultivation of these virtues with his path called the eightfold path: ". . . that practice [namely, the mere cultivation of love, and so forth] is not conducive to turning away, nor to dispassion, nor to quieting, nor to cessation, nor to direct knowledge, nor to enlightenment, nor to Nirvana, but only to rebirth in the world of Brahma.

". . . my practice is conducive to complete turning away, dispassion, cessation, quieting, direct knowledge, enlightenment, and Nirvana—specifically the eightfold noble path."[1] The Buddha is saying that in order to attain enlightenment and salvation, one must couple the practice of morality with the cultivation of wisdom, since wisdom and morality are interrelated. The early Buddhist texts explain how this coupling is to be done: ". . . a monk continually related to [the beings in] one direction with a mind endowed with love; then likewise, [the beings in] the second, the third, and the fourth [direction]; and in the same way [to the beings] upward, downward, and across. He continually related everywhere; equally, to the entire world [of beings], with a mind endowed with love—a mind that is untroubled, free from enmity, vast, enlarged, and measureless. He then reflects in this way; 'Even this liberation of the mind which is love is produced and intended. Whatever is produced, and intended is impermanent, is subject to cessation.' He understands this. He becomes established in this [understanding] and destroys the harmful influences. If he does not destroy the harmful influences, then . . . he destroys the five lower fetters and comes to have spontaneous birth [in a Brahma world]"[2] However, even the exclusive cultivation of these virtues would take one very close to the ultimate realization because these virtues have many salvific or Nirvanic features or characteristics. In the following analysis, I am very much indebted to the admirable analysis of these virtues done by Harvey Aronson in his *Love and Sympathy in Theravada Buddhism*, in which he treats sympathy also as an equally important virtue.

Buddhist Concept of Metta

The Western concept of *agape* (in the sense of fraternal concern) best expresses the meaning of the word *Mettā*, and the practice of *Mettā* plays a major role in Buddhist meditational practice. The Buddha said that one who sustains a loving mind even for the duration of a snap of the fingers accumulates a vast amount of merit and can be truly called a holy person.[3] A loving mind makes one calm and relaxed: "Monks, just the rudimentary level of love, merely relating to sentient beings with (the wish for their) welfare is a cause for breathing easily."[4] This loving mind is to be sustained in all activities, in sitting, eating, walking, *etc.* Even when criticizing another, we should do so with a loving mind. If one wishes to criticize or correct another, one should do so, "at the proper time, speaking truthfully, gently, profitably, and with a loving mind."[5]

Sometimes, loving is explained as a way of identifying with others. Once a group of monks tell the Buddha that they live so harmoniously together like a 'mixture of milk and water' because they offer loving physical, verbal and mental actions to each other both in their presence and absence. The chief of that group of monks, Anuruddha, explains the basic principle behind their actions: "I, having surrendered my own mind, am living only according to the mind of these venerable ones. Lord, we have diverse bodies, but assuredly only one mind" and goes on to say that each one of them takes care of others' things as if they were one's own. For example, if another person has not cleaned his room then one would clean it as if it were one's own room.[6]

A primary function of love is to displace hostility. There are several ways to displace hostility. Before starting the practice of loving-kindness as a meditation, one should sever all impediments to it. Buddhaghosa explains, "To start with, he should review the danger in hate and the advantage in patience . . . and the advantage in patience should be understood according to such *Suttas* as these: 'No higher rule, the Buddhas say, than patience, and no *nibbāña* higher than forbearance' (D. II.49; Dhp. 184). Thereupon he should embark upon the development of loving-kindness for the purpose of secluding the mind from hate (seen as a danger) and introducing it to patience, known as an advantage."[7]

Methods to Displace Resentment

If the resentment towards a person persists, there are several techniques to be applied. One is to think as follows: " 'Just as I want to be happy and dread pain, as I want to live and not to die, so do other beings, too.' Using himself as the example, then the desire for other beings' welfare and happiness arises in him. And this method is indicated by the Blessed One's saying "I visited all quarters with my mind, nor found I any dearer than myself; self is likewise to every other dear; who loves himself will never harm another' (S. I.75; U. 47)."[8]

Buddhaghosa explains another method: "If you are angry now, you will be one who does not carry out the Blessed One's teaching; by repaying an angry man in kind you will be worse than the angry man and not win the battle hard to win; you will yourself do to yourself the things that help your enemy; and you will be like a pyre log."

'. . . As a log from a pyre, burned at both ends and fouled in the middle, serves neither for timber in the village nor for timber in the forest, so is such a person as this, I say' (A. II.95; It. 90).The Buddha once said: "Although a dog would bite a man's leg, the man would not bite the dog's leg (*Yassa yo sā ḍase pādam, tassa pādam no so ḍase*)."

"If his resentment subsides when he strives and makes effort in this way, it is good. If not, then he should remove irritation by remembering some controlled and purified state in that person, which inspires confidence when remembered.

"For one person may be controlled in his bodily behavior with his control in doing an extensive course of duty known to all, though his verbal and mental behavior are not controlled. Then the latter should be ignored and the control in his bodily behavior remembered. . .

"But there may be another in whom not even one of these three things is controlled. Then, compassion for that one should be aroused thus: Although he is going about in the human world now, nevertheless after a certain number of days he will find himself in [one of] the eight hells or the sixteen prominent hells. For irritation also subsides through compassion."[9] "But if it still does not subside in him when he reviews ownership of deeds (karma) in this way, then he should review the special qualities of the Master's former conduct.

"Here is the way of reviewing it: Now you who have gone forth, is it now the fact that when your Master was a Bodhisattva before discovering full enlightenment, while he was still engaged in fulfilling the Perfections during the four incalculable ages and a hundred thousand eons, he did not allow hate to corrupt his mind even when his enemies tried to murder him on various occasions?"[10]

"But if, as he reviews the special qualities of the Master's former conduct, the resentment still does not subside in him, since he has long been used to the slavery of defilement, then he should review the *Suttas* that deal with the beginninglessness [of the round of rebirths]. Here is what is said: '*Bhikkhus*, it is not easy to find a being who has not formerly been your mother . . . your father . . . your brother . . . your sister . . . your son . . . your daughter.' (S. II. 189-90). Consequently, he should think about that person thus: This person, it seems, as my mother in the past carried me in her womb for nine months and removed from me without disgust as if it were yellow sandalwood my urine, excrement, spittle, *etc.*, she played with me in her lap, and nourished me, carrying me about on her hip. And this person as father went by goat paths and paths set on piles, to pursue the merchant trade, and he risked his life for me by going into battle in double array, by sailing on the great ocean in ships, and he nourished me by bringing back wealth by one means or another, thinking to feed his children. And as my brother, sister, son, daughter, this person helped my life. So it is unbecoming for me to harbor hatred for him in my mind.

"But, if he is still unable to quench that thought in this way, then he should review the advantages of loving kindness thus: . . . has it not been said by the Blessed One as follows: "*Bhikkhus*, when the mind-deliverance of loving kindness is cultivated, developed, much practiced, made the vehicle, made the foundation, established, consolidated, and properly undertaken, eleven blessings can be expected. What are the eleven? A man sleeps in comfort, wakes in comfort, and dreams no evil dreams, he is dear to human beings, he is dear to non-human beings, deities guard him, fire and poison and weapons do not affect him, his mind is easily concentrated, the expression of his face is serene, he dies unconfused, if he penetrates no higher he will be reborn in the Brahma World.' (A. V.342) If you do not stop this thought, you will be denied these advantages.

"But, if he is still unable to stop it in this way, he should try resolution into elements. How?. . . when you are angry with him, what is it you are angry with? Is it head hairs you are angry with? or body hairs? or nails? . . . the mind element? Is it the mental-object element or the mind-consciousness element you are angry with? For when he tries the resolution into elements, his anger finds no foothold, like a mustard seed on the point of an awl or a painting on the air.

"But, if he cannot effect the resolution into elements, he should try the giving of a gift. . . . And in the one who does this the annoyance with that person entirely subsides. And in the other even anger that has been dogging him from a past birth subsides at the moment . . .

"When his resentment towards that hostile person has been thus allayed, then he can turn his mind with loving kindness toward that person too, just as towards the one who is dear, the very dear friend, and the neutral person. Then he should break down the barriers by practicing loving kindness over and over again, accomplishing mental impartiality towards the four persons, that is to say, himself, the dear person, the neutral person and hostile person.

“”The characteristic of it is this: Suppose this person is sitting in a place with a dear, a neutral, and a hostile person, himself being the fourth; then bandits come to him and say, ‘Venerable sir, give us a *bhikkhu,*’ and on being asked why, they answer ‘So that we may kill him and use the blood of his throat as an offering,’ then if that *bhikkhu* thinks ‘Let them take this one, or this one,’ he has not broken down the barriers. And also if he thinks ‘Let them take me but not these three,’ he has not broken down the barriers either. Why? Because he seeks the harm of him whom he wishes to be taken and seeks the welfare of the others only. But it is when he does not see a single one among the four people to be given to the bandits and he directs his mind impartially towards himself and towards those three people that he has broken down the barriers.”[11]

The cultivation of love has benefits for the individual in this life itself as well as in the next. We saw above how one gains eleven benefits by practicing love. Buddhism maintains that love or loving can generate beneficial power and this power necessarily protects the lover. “In this context some tell the story of the cow. A cow was standing giving milk to her calf. A hunter, playing with a spear in his hand, thought, “I will hit that [cow]’ He threw the spear, which struck her body but bounced off like a palm leaf. . . . It was due to the fact that she had a strong state of mind [wishing] for the welfare of the calf. Love has great power in this way.”[12] Aronson comments: “Love, compassion, sympathetic joy, and equanimity are not defined in the first four collection of discourses; however, the commentaries and *The Path of Purification* do supply definitions and explanations. Because of the distinctive characteristics of each sublime attitude, it can be understood that when one is present the others are absent. With respect to the nature of love, it ‘has the characteristic of devotion (*pavatti*) to the aspect of others’ welfare’ (*Vsm.* ix.93). ‘It has the function of offering welfare’ (*Vsm.* ix.93). The meditative cultivation of love is particularly effective for counteracting anger (*Vsm.* ix.108).”[13] Now as to the meaning of loving kindness: ‘It is melting (*mejjati*) is the meaning. Also: it comes about with respect to a friend (*mitta*), or it is behavior towards a friend, thus it is loving kindness (*mettā*).[14]

"Compassion 'has the characteristic of devotion to removing [others'] suffering' (*Vsm.* ix.94). 'It has the function of not enduring others' suffering'. The meditative cultivation of compassion is particularly effective for counteracting harmfulness (*Vsm.* ix.108)."[15] "When there is suffering in others it causes (*karoti*) good people's hearts to be moved (*kampana*), thus it is compassion (*karuṇā*). Or alternatively, it combats (*kinati*) others' suffering, attacks and demolishes it, thus it is compassion. Or alternatively, it is scattered (*kirīyati*) upon those who suffer, it is extended to them by pervasion, thus it is compassion (*karuṇā*). . . . it succeeds when it makes cruelty subside."[16] The technique of arousing compassion for an evil person is as follows: "Suppose a robber has been caught with stolen goods, and in accordance with the king's command to execute him, the king's men bind him and lead him off to the place of execution, giving him a hundred blows in sets of four. Then people give him things to chew and eat and also garlands and perfumes, unguents and betel levels. Although he goes along eating and enjoying these things as though he were happy and well off, still no one fancies that he is really happy and well off. On the contrary people feel compassion for him, thinking 'This poor wretch is now about to die; every step he takes brings him nearer to the presence of death.' So too a *bhikkhu* whose meditation subject is compassion should arouse compassion for an [evil-doing] person even if he is happy: 'Though this poor wretch is now happy, cheerful, enjoying his wealth, still for want of even one good deed done now in any one of the three doors [of body, speech and mind] he can come to experience untold suffering in the states of loss.'[17]

"Sympathetic joy 'has the characteristic of rejoicing' (*Vsm.* ix.95). It has the function of being non-envious' (*Vsm.* ix.95). The meditative cultivation of sympathetic joy is particularly effective for counteracting displeasure (*Vsm.* ix.108)."Equanimity" has the characteristic of devotion to the aspect of even-mindedness with regard to sentient beings' (*Vsm.* ix.96). The meditative cultivation of equanimity is particularly effective for counteracting lust (*rāga*) (*Vsm.* ix.108). The sublime *attitude* equanimity is distinct from the *feeling* equanimity; the former is neutrality with regard to sentient beings; the latter is the feeling of neither pleasure nor pain that accompanies various states of consciousness (*Vsm.* iv.158, 162).

"The functions of these four attitudes are stated in terms of what they motivate in an individual. *The Ultimate Light* offers somewhat more evocative definitions and epitomes: 'Love is the state of desiring to offer happiness and welfare with the thought, 'May all beings be happy,' and so forth. Compassion is the state of desiring to remove suffering and misfortune, with the thought, 'May they be liberated from these sufferings,' and so forth. Sympathetic joy is the state of desiring the continuity of [others'] happiness and welfare, with the thought, 'You beings are rejoicing; it is good that you are rejoicing; it is very good,' and so forth. Equanimity is the state of observing [another's] suffering or happiness and thinking 'These appear because of that individual's own past activities' (*Pa.* ii.28)"[18] ". . . loving kindness has the purpose of warding off ill will, while the others have the respective purposes of warding off cruelty, aversion (boredom), and greed or resentment."[19]

"In cultivating love as a sublime attitude, beginners are cautioned against trying to develop it towards members of the opposite sex, as love can too easily become lust (*Vsm.* ix.4,6). The practitioner must always be cautious to root out any traces of attachment, clinging, or bias that might affect his development of love (*Vsm.* ix.93). With care this is possible. The meditator expands the range of his love by progressively cultivating it first toward himself, then toward a respected teacher, a friend, a neutral person and finally a hostile person. He must then equalize, deepen, and extend this attitude—his goal being concentrated universal love, which does not discriminate between self and other (*Vsm.* ix.40-48)."[20] "The divine abiding of loving kindness has greed as its near enemy since both share in seeing virtues. . . . So loving kindness should be well protected from it."[21]

"Similarly, compassion becomes mistaken if sadness arises (*Vsm.* ix.94). Although it is often felt that it is only through becoming sorrowful ourselves that we are truly compassionate to others, this is not so. Compassion consists only of wishing that others be free from suffering. We do not help others by being overcome by their misery. Between heartlessness, on the one hand, and being thoroughly overwhelmed by others' difficulties, on the other, there lies the option of care without grief. The practitioner must be ever alert to remove any sadness that arises during cultivation of compassion. He starts with a person who is suffering intensely and wishes that that person be free from suffering. Then he cultivates it for a dear person, a neutral person, and a hostile person (*Vsm.* ix.80) . . . In order to make compassion a sublime attitude, the practitioner must equalize, strengthen, and universalize it."[22] Compassion is an important driving motive in Buddhist ethics. It is that which makes one feel obliged to go out and help others.

"Sympathetic joy means to take joy in others' success. It becomes mistaken when merriment or giddiness are produced and one is carried away with others' success (*Vsm.* ix.95). Insofar as balance is a necessary factor if there is to be a wholesome mind, any loss of the balance through over-involvement in others' success tends to lead toward unwholesomeness and thus would be a deviation from correct practice. In cultivating sympathetic joy, a person begins with regard to the past, present, or future success of a dear friend (*Vsm.* ix.85). He then progresses to the success of a neutral person and a hostile person. In the subsequent steps he proceeds as in the cases of love and compassion.

"Equanimity is complete evenness of mind in perceiving others' happiness or suffering. It is cultivated only at the level of the fourth absorption (*jhāna*) (*Vsm.* ix.111). Meditators are motivated to cultivate equanimity because they see the disadvantages in the first three sublime attitudes, each of which can be cultivated in any of the first three absorptions (*Vsm.* ix.111). The first three sublime attitudes are conjoined with concern for sentient beings' enjoyments in that they are the wish that beings be happy and so forth (*Vsm.* ix.88). Such a wish is seen as a disadvantage compared to the peace associated with the sublime attitude equanimity which is free from such concern. Furthermore, the first three sublime attitudes are very close to approval and aversion (*Vsm.* ix.88). Love must be guarded lest it change into attachment; compassion, lest it turn into aversion and sadness at others' condition; sympathetic joy, lest it turn into giddiness. These dangers are seen as disadvantages compared to the peacefulness of equanimity, which need not be guarded in this way. Finally, the first three sublime attitudes are associated with the feeling of bliss because they are the means of escaping from enmity, harmfulness, and displeasure, all of which are associated with grief (*Vsm.* ix.88, 111). The bliss that occurs in the first three absorptions is seen as gross compared to the *feeling* equanimity that occurs in conjunction with the sublime *attitude* equanimity in the fourth absorption.

"Equanimity becomes mistaken if it turns into mere unknowing equanimity (*Vsm.* ix.96). Properly cultivated, equanimity involves the realization that others are owners of their activities, and thus their future circumstances will reflect the ethical aspect of their current activities (*Vsm.* ix.96). While virtue leads to welcome consequences, non-virtue brings the opposite (*Vsm.* ix.23-24). Others must ultimately take the responsibility for their own fate; the practitioner, for his. Mindful of this, the meditator frees his mind from all unwholesome approval and aversion towards others' conduct and sustains wholesome impartiality. . ."[23]

Buddhaghosa explains why the sublime virtues are termed divine abidings: "The divineness of the abiding (*brahmavihāratā*) should be understood here in the sense of best and in the sense of immaculate. For these abidings are the best in being the right attitude towards beings." And these virtues are the correct path to purity: "For among these, loving-kindness is the way to purity for one who has much ill will; compassion is that for one who has much cruelty; gladness [sympathetic joy] is that for one who has much aversion (boredom); and equanimity is that for one who has much greed. Also attention given to beings is only fourfold, that is to say, as bringing welfare, as removing suffering, as being glad at their success, and as unconcern, [that is to say, impartial neutrality]. And one abiding in the Measureless States should practice loving-kindness and the rest like a mother with four sons, namely, a child, an invalid, one in the flush of youth, and one busy with his own affairs; for she wants the child to grow up, wants the invalid to get well, wants the one in the flush of youth to enjoy for long the benefits of youth, and is not at all bothered about the one who is busy with his own affairs."[24]

Aronson maintains that sympathy (*anukampā*) is equal in importance to the four sublime virtues. The Buddha's sympathy had something unique about it. "Buddha's motive for teaching others was a very special kind of sympathy. He was neither overcome nor bound by it. In the *Kindred Sayings*, Gotama [the Buddha] makes this point to the spirit Sakka: 'Sakka, a wise individual would not sympathize [with others] out of the same motives which bring others together. If one with a clear mind instructs another, he is not bound through it, by this sympathy, or by his tender care' (*S.* i.206). The bonds of fondness and attachment that bring worldly individuals together influence their sympathy. However, Gotama's interest in others' happiness was free from all normal worldly bias and attachment, and thus, it was unbounded. He was not fettered by helping others' progress."[25] The Buddha's sympathy was expedient, even though it may be unpleasant. For example, if a wooden chip gets stuck in a child's throat, a parent may have to inflict some pain on the child to take it out.[26]

Love is epitomized by the wish that all beings be happy; "compassion is epitomized with the corresponding wish that they be free from suffering" (*Pa. ii.128*). "Sympathy is a general, not a technical term, nor is it the object of the verb 'cultivate' (*bhaveti*) as in meditations. It is the fraternal concern that is present in an individual and does not require cultivation of meditative development."[27] The most important expression of the monks' sympathy is their teaching.

Sympathy is the best antidote to enmity and anger. When one actually becomes hostile, one then tries to call to mind a pure activity that the other person has performed, and Aronson says, "this stands as a challenge to those who assert that constraint of unwholesome attitudes necessarily leads to mental or physical damage."[28]

6

The Origin and Nature of Society

To appreciate the full significance of the Buddhist view of society, we must briefly look at the prevalent social philosophy prior to the time of the Buddha. The dominant philosophical religious tradition at the time was Hinduism and it had a very static view of society. It held that the existing society and the social order was divinely created by Brahma. It is stated in the *Puruṣa Sūkta* of the *Ṛg Veda* that at the beginning of creation, Brahma assumed the form of a Great Being (*Puruṣa*) and the four classes or castes were created from the body of this *Puruṣa*: "His mouth was the Brahamin, his two arms were made the warrior, his two thighs the *Vaiśyā*; from his two feet the *Śudra* was born." The most dangerous and morally disastrous teaching of this doctrine was the divine sanctification of the caste system by birth. As the social order was divinely ordained, it was a sin against Brahma to challenge or change that order. Therefore, the society was considered static and non-evolving. Reinforcing this structure further, they maintained that the king was the manifestation of a divine being in human form (*Mahatī devatā esā, nara rūpena tiṣṭhati*). Therefore, to challenge the king was to challenge the divine authority itself. It was against such a view of society that the Buddha preached an evolutionary doctrine of society and man.

The *Aggañña Sutta*[1] explains this evolution in terms of a mythical story. The Buddha, adressing a Brahamin called Vāseṭṭha, says, "sooner or later, after the lapse of a long, long period, this world passes away. And when this happens, beings have mostly been born in the World of Radiance; and there they dwell, made of mind, feeding on rapture, self-luminous, traversing the air, continuing in glory, and thus they remain for a long, long period of time. There comes also a time, Vāseṭṭha, when sooner or later this world begins to re-evolve. When this happens, beings who had deceased from the World of Radiance, usually come to life as humans. And they become made of mind, feeding on rapture, self- luminous, traversing the air, continuing in glory, and remain thus for a long, long period of time.

"Now at that time, all had become one world of water, dark, and of darkness that maketh blind. No moon nor sun appeared, no stars were seen, nor constellations, neither was night manifest nor day, neither months nor half-months, neither years nor seasons, neither female nor male. Beings were reckoned just as beings only. And to those beings, Vāseṭṭha, sooner or later after a long time, earth with its savor was spread out in the waters. Even as a scum forms on the surface of boiled milky rice that is cooling, so did the earth appear. It became endowed with color, with odor, and with taste. Even as well-made ghee or pure butter, so was its color; even as the flawless honey of the bee, so sweet was it.

"Then, Vāseṭṭha, some being of greedy disposition, said: Lo now! what will this be? and tasted the savory earth with his finger. He thus, tasting, became suffused with the savor, and craving entered into him. And other beings, following his example, tasted the savory earth with their fingers. Thus tasting, they became suffused with the savor, a craving entered into them. Then those beings began to feast on the savory earth, breaking off lumps of it with thier hands. And from the doing thereof the self-luminance of those beings faded away. As their self-luminance faded away, the moon and the sun became manifest. Thereupon star-shapes and constellations became manifest. Thereupon night and day became manifest, months too and half- months, the seasons and the year. Thus far then, Vāseṭṭha, did the world evolve again."

The Central Immorality

It is significant to note the central part played by craving here. According to Buddhism, craving is the central immorality and this practice of immorality leads individuals to their mental and physical deterioration. The other noteworthy feature seen in this Sutta is the close relationship between morality and nature. Nature responds to morality and the gradual increase of the practice of immorality leads to gradual deterioration of the physical nature or atmosphere around these beings.

"Now those beings, Vāseṭṭha, feasting on the savory earth, feeding on it, nourished by it, continued thus for a long, long while. And in measure as they thus fed, did their bodies became solid, and did variety in their comeliness become manifest. Some beings were well-favored, some were ill-favored. And herein they that were well-favored despised them that were ill-favored, thinking: We are more comely than they; they are worse favored than we. And while they through pride in their beauty thus became vain and conceited, the savory earth disappeared. At the disappearance of the savory earth, they gathered themselves together and bewailed it: Alas for the savor! alas for the savor! . . . Then, Vāseṭṭha, when the savory earth had vanished for those beings, outgrowths appeared in the soil. The manner of the rising up thereof was as the springing up of the mushroom, it had color, odor and taste; even as well-formed ghee or fine butter so was the color thereof, and even as flawless honeycomb so was the sweetness thereof. Then those beings began to feast on these outgrowths of the soil. And they, feasting on them, finding food and nourishment in them, continued for a long, long while. And in measure as they thus fed and were thus nourished, so did their bodies grow ever more solid, and the difference in their comeliness more manifest, some becoming well-favored, some ill-favored. Then they that were well-favored despised them that were ill-favored, thinking: We are more comely than they; they are worse favored than we. And while they, through pride in their beauty, thus became vain and conceited, these outgrowths of the soil disappeared. Thereupon creeping plants appeared, and the manner of the growth thereof was as that of the bamboo, and they had color, odor and taste. Even as well-made ghee or fine butter so was the color thereof; even as flawless honeycomb so was the sweetness thereof.

"Then, Vāseṭṭha, those beings began to feast on the creepers. And they, feasting on them, feeding on them, nourished by them, continued so for a long, long while. And in measure as they thus fed and were nourished did their bodies wax more solid, and the divergence in their comeliness increase, so that, as before, the better favored despised the worse favored. And while those, through pride in their beauty, became vain and conceited, the creepers disappeared. At the disappearance thereof they gathered themselves together and bewailed, saying: Verily it was ours, the creeper! Now it has vanished away! . . .

"Then, Vāseṭṭha, when the creepers had vanished for those beings, rice appeared ripening in open spaces, . . . Where they gathered and carried away rice for supper one evening, the next morning the rice stood ripe and grown again. Where they gathered and carried away rice for breakfast in the morning, there in the evening it stood ripe and grown again. No break was to be seen: where the husks had been broken off.

"Then those beings feasting on this rice in the clearings, feeding on it, nourished by it, so continued for a long, long while. And in measure as they, thus feeding, went on existing, so did the bodies of those beings become even more solid, and the divergence in their comeliness more pronounced. In the female appeared the distinctive features of the female, in the male those of the male. Then truly did woman contemplate man too closely, and man, woman. In them contemplating over much the one the other, passion arose and burning entered their bodies. They in consequence thereof, followed their lusts. And beings seeing them so doing threw some sand, some ashes, some cow dung [at them], crying, "Perish, foul one! perish, foul one! How can a being treat a being so? . . .

"That which was reckoned immoral at that time, Vāseṭṭha, is now reckoned to be moral. Those beings who at that time followed their lusts, were not allowed to enter village or town either for a whole month or even for two months. And inasmuch as those beings at that time quickly incurred blame for immorality, they set to work to make huts, to conceal just that immorality."

Development of Social Complications

This shows how the basic elements of the social structure like the family come into being due to the conception of the egoistic feelings like privacy and greed which are, also, the results of lust or craving. Thus the separation of individuals into social units is due to a basic immorality. This separation makes the social situation more complex and leads to further social complications.

"Then Vāseṭṭha, this occured to some being of a lazy disposition: Lo now! why do I wear myself out fetching rice for supper in the evening, and in the morning for breakfast? What if I were to fetch enough rice for supper and breakfast together? So he gathered at one journey enough rice for the two meals together.

"Then some being came to him and said: Come, good being, let us go rice-gathering. That is not wanted, good being, I have fetched rice for the evening and morning meal. Then the former followed his example and fetched rice for two days at once, saying: So much, they say, will about do. Then some other being came to this one and said: Come, good being, let us go rice-gathering. And he: Never mind, good being, I have fetched rice enough for two days. (And so, in like manner, they stored up rice enough for four, and then for eight days.)

"Now from the time, Vāseṭṭha, that those beings began to feed on hoarded rice, powder enveloped the clean grain, and husk enveloped the grain, and the reaped or cut stems did not grow again, a break became manifest (where the reaper had cut); the rice-stubble stood in clumps.

"Now some being, Vāseṭṭha, of greedy disposition, watching over his own plot, stole another plot and made use of it. They took him and holding him fast, said: Truly, good being, thou hast wrought evil in that, while watching thine own plot, thou hast stolen another plot and made use of it. See, good being, that thou do not such a thing again! Ay, Sirs, he replied. And a second time he did so. And yet a third. And again they took him and admonished him. Some smote him with the hand, some with clods, some with sticks. With such a beginning, Vāseṭṭha, did stealing appear, and censure and lying and punishment became known." Thus, due to the scarcity of rice, boundaries to rice fields appear, and with the appearance of private property, a new set of vices like stealing arises. In Buddhism, private property is regarded as a very basic evil. Monks are strictly advised not to possess any private property except the basic minimums like the bowl and clothing. The ideas in the *Sutta* are significant in the way they show the intimate relationship between material conditions and the human psyche. The Buddha strongly emphasized the interaction between matter and mind. It is interesting to note that in discussing the twelve-linked law of dependent origination, the relationship between consciousness (*viññāṇa*) and name and form (*nāmarūpa*) is often singled out to emphasize their interaction when their relationship is formulated in both ways (*aññamaññapaccaya*): "name and form originate depending on consciousness, and consciousness originates depending on name and form (*viññāṇapaccayā nāmarūpaṃ, nāmarūpapaccayā viññāṇaṃ*)." In the standard formula, consciousness is always given priority because it is the consciousness that ultimately fabricates matter. Therefore, in a sense, the mind is prior. But what happens, in the process, is that the very matter which the consciousness fabricated starts enslaving the consciousness. As Ñāṇananda explained above, what happens here is a clear case of the servant becoming the master. So we must realize that the very matter that is affecting us was fabricated by ourselves. This *Sutta* graphically illustrates how the mental changes lead to the creation of material changes and how, later on, those material changes lead to the creation of mental changes. Therefore Buddhism advocates the need and usefulness of bringing about material changes in order to effect changes in the psychic structure of human beings.

Social Changes and Psychic Changes

Another important fact explained in this *Sutta* is that any given social structure is a mental creation of the society which constitutes it. Social changes happen basically due to psychic changes. These psychic changes have so far been immoral, being dominated by the three basic defilements: greed, hatred and ignorance. Institutionalized social structures are evil because they are all attempts to make compromises with evil. In the ordinary society, social institutions have become a necessary evil and they lead to further immoralities like lying, stealing and punishment. An individual who throws away the basic evils, or defilements, greed, hatred and ignorance, goes beyond or transcends the level of social institutions and therefore he is called a person "who is not attached to institutions" (*kulesu ananugiddho*).[2] Buddha further explains in this *Sutta* how the society coped with this evil social situation by appointing a righteous king to direct and guide them in the best moral way possible.

"Now those beings, Vāseṭṭha, gathered themselves together, and bewailed these things, saying: From our evil deeds, Sirs, becoming manifest, inasmuch as stealing, censure, lying, punishment have become known, what if we were to select a certain being, who should be wrathful when indignation is right, who should censure that which should rightly be censured and should banish him who deserves to be banished. But we will give him in return a proportion of the rice.

"Then, Vāseṭṭha, those beings went to the being among them who was the handsomest, the best favored, the most attractive, the most capable and said to him Come now, good being, be indignant at that which one should rightly be indignant, censure that which should rightly be censured, banish him who deserves to be banished. And we will contribute to thee a proportion of our rice. And he consented, and did so, and they gave him a proportion of their rice.

"Chosen by the whole people, Vāseṭṭha, is what is meant by *Mahā Sammata*; so *Mahā Sammata* (the Great Elect) was the first standing phrase to arise (for such one)." This passage also illustrates the Buddhist conception of the origin of society and of kingship. The king is a ruler elected by the consensus of the people, responsible to them. Thus Buddhism believes in a social contract theory of the origin of the state and of society.

In contradiction to the Hindu theory of caste, the Buddha goes on to say that the four classes of people, *Brahamins*, *Khattiyas*, *Vessas* and *Suddas*, did not become so because they were so created by Brahma, but simply because of their professions. "Now, Vāseṭṭha, there were some others of those beings who, adopting the married state, set on foot various trades. That they, adopting the married state, set on foot various trades (*vissa*) is, Vāseṭṭha, the meaning of *Vessa* (tradesfolk). So this word came into use as a standing expression for such people." And those that adopted hunting became the *Suddas* or *Śūdras*.

And also, the *Sutta* states that there is no intrinsically rigid hierarchy among these classes because it could change in differing historical contexts. Referring to the social class of Brahamins at the early stage of society, the Buddha says, "at that time they were looked upon as the lowest; now they are thought the best." Thus Buddhism gives an empirical and a social theory about the evolution of class structure as opposed to the Hindu metaphysical theory of the divine origin of the classes or castes.

7

Buddhist Social Ethics

During the time of the Buddha, the Brahamin dominance and the caste system were so rigid in the Hindu social order, that the *Śūdras* were completely degraded as a kind of non-human life-form. As Ghurye observes, "Manu declares roundly that a *Śūdra* cannot commit an offence causing loss of his caste, so degraded was he."[1] As Jayatilleke and Malalasekara explain, all basic human cvil rights were denied to them. They were denied the equality of political opportunity. "Even if a *Śūdra* mentions the name and class of the twice-born arrogantly, an iron nail ten fingers long shall be thrust red hot into his mouth."[2] They were denied the equality of economic opportunity. *The Laws of Manu* says, "A *Śūdra*, whether bought or unbought, may be compelled to do servile work; for he was created by the Self-Existent to be the slave of a Brahamin."[3] They were denied the equality of social opportunity . . . A Brahamin "who instructs *Śūdra* pupils" was penalized.[4] ". . . free access to wells and sometimes even the use of roads was denied to them."[5] *Śūdra* were denied religious freedom. "Not only was the *Śūdra* denied access to religious instruction, he had no right, unlike the 'superior' castes (*i.e.*,

Brahamins, Kṣatriyas and *Vaiśyas*), to be initiated[6] or to have religious ceremonies performed for him."[7] And lastly, the *Śūdra* were denied equality before the law. "A *Śūdra* commiting homicide or theft suffered confiscation of his property and capital punishment,[8] but a Brahamin was only blinded for such crimes."[9] It was in this social context that the Buddha preached his social philosophy.

Buddhist Emphasis on Equality

It is important to realize that the Buddha was the first religious thinker in history to emphasize the equality of humanity. He firmly stated this by insisting that "the four classes are equal to one another" (*Cattāro vaṇṇā samasamā*).[10] In most other religions in the world, and in all religions prior to the Buddha, there is always a conception of an "elite" or a superior group. Towards the end of the *Aggañña Sutta*, the Buddha shows how people from all classes could enter the Buddhist order of monks.[11] Here he gives two strong arguments to prove the equality of the human race. The first is that before the moral law, persons of all four classes are completely equal. Whether a *Brahamin* or a *Śūdra*, if one does bad actions one will reap bad results.[12] The second argues that human beings are all equally capable of attaining ultimate enlightenment, there being no difference at all in their spiritual capacities and therefore are all equal before the Law of Spiritual Development.[13]

Elsewhere the Buddha gives further arguments against racism and caste differences, and in support of the equality of mankind. As Jayatilleke and Malalasekara state, the Buddha argues "on biological grounds that: unlike in the case of plant and animal kingdoms, where differences of species are noticeable—mankind is one species."[14] "Arguing from the reality of free will and the capacity that man has within himself of becoming either moral or immoral or even happy or unhappy by transforming himself or degenerating morally as the case may be, the Buddha denies that there are such fixed human types genetically determined. There are no men who are intrinsically good or evil by nature and must necessarily remain so, for the evil can turn into good and the good degenerate into evil. . . . The emphasis is not on what a man is born with, but what he does with himself, since man, irrespective of his physical constitution and psychological nature at birth, can—given the opportunity and effort—change for better or worse."[15] "As the Mahayana texts put it, it is not only men but all sentient beings down to the very lowest who are potential Buddhas, in that a Buddha-nature (*Buddha-bhāva*) is present within them. If only for this reason, no one has a right to despise a fellow creature, since all are subject to the same laws of existence and have ultimately the same nature and the same potentialities, though they are in varying stages of growth or development, and their rates of growth may differ from time to time."[16]

Buddha's Advice to Sigāla

The *Sigālovāda Sutta* is regarded as an important statement of Buddhist social ethics. When the Buddha meets Sigāla, a Hindu householder, the latter is seen practicing the holy rite of worshipping the six quarters and says that the proper worship of the six quarters is to engage in moral practice. He talks to Sigāla: "Inasmuch, young householder, as the *Ariyan* disciple has put away the four vices in conduct, inasmuch as he does no evil actions from the four motives, inasmuch as he does not pursue the six channels for dissipating wealth, he thus, avoiding these fourteen evil things, is a coverer of the six quarters; he has practiced so as to conquer both worlds; he tastes success both in this world and in the next. At the dissolution of the body, after death, he is reborn to a happy destiny in heaven. What are the four vices of conduct that he has put away? The destruction of life, the taking what is not given, licentiousness, and lying speech. These are the four vices of conduct that he has put away. . . . By which four motives does he do no evil deed? Evil deeds are done from motives of partiality, enmity, stupidity and fear. But inasmuch as the Ariyan disciple is not led away by these motives, he through them does no evil deed."[17]

The Buddha appeals to common sense in showing the evils of immoral practices, and he shows the paradoxical evil results of some social pursuits. For example, he says that in gambling one is always logically bound to lose because if one wins then one is hated by others, and if one loses then one is sad about what one lost. It is interesting to note also that the Buddha regarded idleness as a moral evil.

"Which are the six channels for dissipating wealth? Being addicted to intoxicating liquors, frequenting the streets at unseemly hours, haunting fairs, being infatuated by gambling, associating with evil companions, the habit of idleness.

"There are, young householder, these six dangers through the being addicted to intoxicating liquors: actual loss of wealth, increase of quarrels, susceptibility of disease, loss of good character, indecent exposure, impaired intelligence.

"Six, young householder, are the perils from frequenting the streets at unseemly hours: he himself is without guard and protection and so also are wife and children; so also is his property; he moreover becomes suspected [as the doer] of crimes, and false rumors fix on him, and many are the troubles he goes out to meet.

"Six, young householder, are the perils from the haunting of fairs: [He is ever thinking] Where is there dancing? Where is there singing? Where is there music? Where is recitation? Where are the cymbals? Where the tam-tams?

"Six, young householder, are the perils for him who is infatuated with gambling: as winner he begets hatred; when beaten he mourns his lost wealth; his actual substance is wasted; his word has no weight in a court of law; he is despised by friends and officials; he is not sought after by those who would give or take in marriage, for they would say that a man who is a gambler cannot afford to keep a wife.

"Six, young householder, are the perils from associating with evil companions: any gambler, any libertine, any tippler, any cheat, any swindler, any man of violence is his friend and companion.

"Six, young householder, are the perils of the habit of idleness: he says, it is too cold, and does no work. He says, 'I am too hungry' and does no work . . . 'too full', and does no work. And while all that he should do remains undone, new wealth he does not get, and such wealth as he has dwindles away . . ."[18]

Sleeping when the sun has arisen, sleeping by day, prowling around at night, entanglement in strife, doing harm, friendship with wicked men, hardness of heart, playing with dice, drinking strong drinks and going to women 'dear as life to other men,' are said to be causes that bring ruin to a man.[19]

As we explained above, Buddhism emphasizes the need for friends. Good friendship (*kalyāṇamittatā*) is said to be of the most fortunate and greatest possessions one can have. Therefore, the Buddha goes into detail to describe the nature of friends and the criteria of a good friend. "Four, O young householder, are they who should be reckoned as foes in the likeness of friends; to wit, a rapacious person, the man of words not deeds, the flatterer, the fellow-waster.

"Of these, the first is on four grounds to be reckoned as a foe in the likeness of a friend: he is rapacious; he gives little and asks much; he does his duty out of fear; he pursues his own interests.

"On four grounds the man of words, not deeds, is to be reckoned as a foe in the likeness of a friend: he makes friendly profession as regards the past: he makes friendly profession as regards the future; he tries to gain your favor by empty sayings; when the opportunity for service has arisen he avows his disability.

"On four grounds the flatterer is to be reckoned as a foe in the likeness of a friend: he both consents to do wrong, and dissents from doing right; he praises you to your face; he speaks ill of you to others.

"On four grounds the fellow-waster companion is to be reckoned as a foe in the likeness of a friend he is your companion when you indulge in strong drinks; he is your companion when you frequent the streets at untimely hours; he is your companion when you haunt shows and fairs; he is your companion when you are infatuated with gambling.

"Four, O young householder, are the friends who should be reckoned as sound at heart: the helper; the friend who is the same in happiness and adversity; the friend of good counsel; the friend who sympathizes.

"On four grounds the friend who is a helper is to be reckoned as sound at heart: he guards you when you are off your guard, he guards your property when you are off your guard; he is a refuge to you when you are afraid; when you have tasks to perform he provides a double supply [of what you may need].

"On four grounds the friend who is the same in happiness and adversity is to be reckoned as sound at heart: he tells you his secrets; he keeps secret your secrets; in your troubles he does not forsake you;

he lays down even his life for your sake.

"On four grounds the friend of good counsel who declares what you need to do is . . . sound at heart: he restrains you from doing wrong; he enjoins you to[do what is] right; he informs you of what you had not heard before; he reveals to you the way to heaven.

"On four grounds the friend who sympathizes is to be reckoned as sound at heart he does not rejoice over your misfortunes; he rejoices over your prosperity; he restrains anyone who is speaking ill of you; he commends anyone who is praising you."[20]

Sympathy plays an important part in good friendship, and the Buddha says that the relationship between friends should be similar to his example of the archetypal perfect moral relationship between mother and child: "The friend who is a helpmate, and the friend of bright days and of dark, and he who shows what it is you need, and he who throbs for you with sympathy: these four the wise should know as friends, and should devote himself to them as a mother to her own, her bosom's child."[21]

The Buddha gives homely advice as to how one should manage one's personal budget. He says that one should divide one's earnings into four portions: one portion to spend and enjoy; two portions to be put back into business, and the fourth portion to be saved for emergencies.[22]

Six Main Social Classes

Referring to the six quarters again, the Buddha says that the real way to respect the six quarters is to pay correct respect to the six main classes in the society. It is significant to note that the Buddha never thought of the possibility of a classless society. For him a classless society is even logically impossible, because in any given social situation, a class structure is necessarily there. It is the inevitable nature of human society. Even if one transcends the class structure of the lay society by entering into the order of monks, even there a class structure based on spiritual development and/or seniority is always evident, and the Buddha considered that to be the perfect class structure. Therefore, for Buddhism there is nothing wrong with class structures as such. What is important is the way the classes interact.

However, the Buddha says that classes should have reciprocal moral relationships with each other. As explained in chapter two, every person, by being in the society, belongs to a particular place in its structure. By being there, he owes some duties to the other related classes. Because he owes duties to the other classes, the other classes owe duties towards him, and those duties become his rights. So, duties and rights imply each other. It is only in the perfect working of the network of rights and duties that a good society could be founded. "And how, O young householder, does the *Ariyan* disciple protect the six quarters? The following should be looked upon as the six quarters: parents as the East, teachers as the South, wife and children as the West, friends and companions as the North, servants and working people as the nadir, religious teachers and Brahamins as the zenith."[23] About the symbolism used here, Rhys Davids says, "The symbolism is deliberately chosen as the day in the East, so life begins with parents' care; teachers' fees and the South are the same word: *dakkhiṇa*; domestic cares follow when the youth becomes man, as the West holds the later day-light; North is 'beyond,' so by help of friends, *etc.*, he gets beyond troubles."[24]

It is significant that in explaining the nature of these relationships the Buddha takes great care to emphasize the subtle, but very significant, needs and behaviors of human beings. For example, the husband should take care to give "jewelry and adornment" to his wife, and an employer should cultiveate intimate feelings with the employees "by sharing unusual delicacies with them."

"In five ways a child should minister to his parents as the Eastern quarter: Once supported by them I will now be their support; I will perform duties incumbent on them; I will keep up the lineage and tradition of my family; I will make myself worthy of my heritage.

"In five ways, parents thus ministered to as the Eastern quarter by their child, show their love for him: they restrain him from vice, they exhort him to virtue, they train him to a profession, they contract a suitable marriage for him, and in due time they hand over his inheritance.

"In five ways should pupils minister to their teachers as the Southern quarter: by rising [from their seat, in salutation], by waiting upon them, by eagerness to learn, by personal service, and by attention when receiving their teaching.

"And in five ways do teachers, thus ministered to as the Southern quarter by their pupils, love their pupil: they train him in that wherein he has been well trained; they make him hold fast that which is well held; they thoroughly instruct him in the lore of every art; they speak well of him among his friends and companions. They provide for his safety in every quarter.

"In five ways should a wife as Western quarter be ministered to by her husband: by respect, by courtesy, by faithfulness, by handing over authority to her, by providing her with adornment.

"In these five ways does the wife, ministered to by her husband as the Western quarter, love him: her duties are well performed, by hospitality to the kin of both, by faithfulness, by watching over the goods he brings, and by skill and industry in discharging all her business.

"In five ways should a clansman minister to his friends and familiars as the Northern quarter: by generosity, courtesy and benevolence, by treating them as he treats himself, and by being as good as his word.

"In these five ways thus ministered to as the Northern quarter, his friends and familiars love him: they protect him when he is off his guard, and on such occasions guard his property, they become a refuge in danger, they do not forsake him in his troubles, and they show consideration for his family.

"In five ways does an *Ariyan* master minister to his servants and employees as the nadir: by assigning them work according to their strength; by supplying them with food and wages; by tending them in sickness; by sharing with them unusual delicacies; by granting leave at times, (*i.e.* for constant relaxation so that they need not work all day, and special leave with extra food and adornment—Commentary).

"In these ways ministered by their master, servants and employees love their master in five ways: they rise before him, they lie down to rest after him; they are content with what is given to them; they do their work well; and they carry about his praise and good fame.

"In five ways should the clansman minister to recluses and Brahamins as the zenith: by affection in act and speech and mind; by keeping open house to them, by supplying their temporal needs.

"Thus ministered to as the zenith, recluses and Brahamins show their love for the clansman in six ways: they restrain him from evil, they exhort him to good, they love him with kindly thoughts: they teach him what he had not heard, they reveal to him the way to heaven."[25]

Moral Principles and Social Order

The Buddha concludes that it is the working of moral principles that can keep the society going in good order. "The giving hand, the kindly speech, the life of service, impartiality to one another, as the case demands; these be the things that make the world go round as linchpin serves the rolling of the car. And if these things be not, no mother reaps the honor and respect her child should pay, nor doth the father win them through the child. And since the wise rightly appraise these things, they win to eminence and earn men's praise."[26]

The *Parābhava Sutta* (The Discourse on the Causes of Downfall) explains that immorality (*adhamma*) leads one to loss while morality leads to winning or success. It goes on to clarify further social immoralities.[27] "The man who is drowsy, fond of society and without energy, lazy, given to anger—that is a cause of loss." The Buddha attaches great significance to the caring of old parents. "He who being rich does not support mother or father who are old or past their youth—that is a cause of loss." Miserliness is condemned, and elsewhere the Buddha has said that "what is left is what is given and what one keeps, stinks. . . The man who is possessed of much property, who has gold and food, [and still] enjoys alone his sweet things . . . The man who is pround of his birth, of his wealth, and of his family, despises his relatives—that is a cause of loss." He refers to common motives for immoralities and their disastrous results. "He who, not satisfied with his own wife, is seen with harlots and the wives of others . . . The man who, past his youth, brings home a woman with breasts like the timbaru fruit, and for jealousy of her cannot sleep—that is a cause of loss." Lastly, the Buddha says that too much ambition is another cause of loss: "He who has little property, [but] great desire, is born in a *Khattiya* family and wishes for the kingdom in this world—that is a cause of loss."

The Buddha redefines the 'outcaste' as an immoral person and the *Vasala Sutta* (The Discourse on the Outcaste) maintains that a person becomes an outcaste not by birth, as the Hindus say, but by doing immoral actions: "Not by birth does one become an outcaste, not by birth does one become a Brahamin; by deeds one becomes an outcaste, by deeds one becomes a Brahamin."[28] In this *Sutta* the emphasis is more on social obligations. "Be it in the village or in the wood, whosoever appropriates by theft what is the property of others and what has not been given, let one know him as an outcaste. . . . Whosoever, having really contracted a debt, runs away when called upon [to pay], saying, 'There is no debt [that I owe] thee,' let one know him as an outcaste. . . . Whosoever, having committed a bad deed, hopes [saying], 'Let no one know me'[as having done it, who is] a dissembler . . . Whosoever, having gone to another's house and partaken of his good food, does not in return honor him when he comes . . . Whosoever, exalts himself and despises others, being mean by his pride—let one know him as an outcaste . . . Whosoever without being a saint pretends to be a saint, he is indeed the lowest outcaste."

Elsewhere, the Buddha places emphasis on shame (*hiri*) and fear of blame (*ottappa*) and calls them the guardians of the world. These are supposed to be two great wealths one could possess. Shame is seen when one reproaches oneself for an evil done (because one can never get away from oneself) or about to be done, and when one has an inward fear derived from thinking of the unpleasant results to be experienced from that action. Here the Buddha refers to the moral and existential significance of the conscience. Fear of blame tends to restrain one from committing immoral actions that are condemned by the society, wise people and/or superiors. Therefore, immoral actions necessarily lead to internal tension, anxiety and worry.

The *Maṅgala Sutta* (Discourse on Blessings) discusses the basic positive virtues.[29] The Sutta starts when a deity approaches the Buddha requesting him to state what is holy or blessed because during the Buddha's time, various religious thinkers claimed various ritual actions to be holy, such as bathing in the Ganges River. Answering the question, the Buddha defines "the blessed and the holy" completely in terms of morality. The *Sutta* starts with "good friendship" as the first blessing. In Buddhism, the highest criteria for individual superiority are placed on spiritual development. Therefore, such people should be respected and worshipped. He praises "vast learning, mastery in skills, a highly trained discipline and pleasant speech."

Filial piety plays a central role in Buddhist society; the Buddha's oft-quoted example for the ideal human relationship is the one between mother and child. Once the Buddha said that "parents are the Brahmas" (*brahmāti mātā pitaro*) and the Buddhist tradition emphasizes that "the mother is the Buddha at home," because the relationship of the mother to her child is exactly like the Buddha's relationship to beings. The Buddhist tradition says that one owes an unconditional obligation to one's mother, however many wrongs she may have done, simply because she underwent so much travail in keeping one within her womb for nine long months and then in undergoing birth pangs. It is interesting to see the tradition emphasizing the mother (not the father) as the Buddha at home. And the children's respect and obligation to their mother should be exactly the same as towards the Buddha. In Buddhism, the father is not as important as the mother, because she has performed the unique feat of giving birth to one's unique chance of living this life.

To the layman, a strong commitment to his family is recommended. "Supporting one's father and mother, cherishing wife and children, being well organized in one's occupation, are called the highest blessing."

Next, the Buddha praises generosity, which can be called the most basic and central Buddhist social virtue. As we explained above, charity or *Dāna* could be a powerful means to achieve the desired ends both at the karmic level and the path level and could be performed at either of these levels. In a way, one could say that in Buddhism *Dāna* is the ultimate ethical action, because it gradually leads towards the cultivation of egolessness. A *Jātaka* story held in high esteem in Buddhist countries is the *Vessantara Jātaka* where the Bodhisattva, as an heir to a kingdom, gives away all his riches and at last gives away his wife and two children, too.

It is important to note that the Buddha states that in choosing one's occupation, one should choose "faultless or morally uncomplicated occupations" (*anākula ca kammantā*) and one should perform only blameless actions (*anavajjāni kammāni*). "Restraint in taking intoxicating drinks" (*majjapanā ca saññamo*) and "diligence in things" (*appamādo ca dhammesu*) are equally important virtues. Buddhism attaches importance to 'humility' as a social virtue: firstly, because it is born out of the understanding that things, including myself, are interdependent, that I owe my existence to everything around me, and therefore, that I owe a great respect to everything; secondly, humility leads to the deflation of the ego, and that takes one towards the realization of egolessness.

Gratitude is related to humility. The Buddha once said that "it is very rare to find people who possess the feeling of gratitude" (*kataññūkatavedī puggalo dullabho lokasmiṃ*). He illustrated his idea of gratitude by a unique example which also illustrates the Buddhist attitude to trees and nature in general. He attained enlightenment under the *Bodhi* tree, and he felt so grateful towards the tree for helping him, that soon after enlightenment he stood looking at the tree for seven days as a way of showing gratitude and respect for the tree.

"Patience, obedience, seeing holy men, and taking part in spiritual discussions at proper times" are also praised as highest blessings. Thus the *Maṅgala Sutta* portrays a description of the basic social virtues needed for the ideal functioning of a social order. The *Sutta* mentions the last blessing as "self-control and seeing the basic noble truths" and ends by giving the ultimate criteria of the perfect blessing: "If one's mind is sorrowless, stainless, and secure and does not shake when touched by worldly vicissitudes, that is the highest blessing."

Another social virtue emphasized is "the awareness of proportion or limit" (*mattaññutā*). One should have a sense of proportion or balance. The Buddha degrades gluttony in enjoyments. He once said with regard to food, that one should stop eating when one feels that only four more mouthfuls can be eaten. We can get an idea of what the Buddha meant if we examine his advice to monks as to their proper attitude towards food. Before partaking of any food, a monk should think as follows: "Wisely reflecting, I will partake of food not for the pleasure of it, not for the pride [resulting from physical strength obtainable], not for adornment, nor for beautifying the body, but merely to maintain this body, to still the hunger, and to enable the practice of the holy life; also to resist the pangs of hunger [due to previous want of food]. Thus will my life be maintained free from wrongdoing[*i.e.* not taking food is wrong because it harms the body] and free from discomfort."[30]

The Buddha condemns careless exploitation of nature and recommends using resources of nature with a sense of respect. This is illustrated by the Buddha's advice as to the way a monk should obtain alms from villagers: "A holy man should make alms rounds in the villages in the way a bee takes the honey from a flower without disturbing the flower's color and smell (*Yathāpi bhamaro pupphaṃ vaṇṇa gandhaṃ aheṭhayaṃ, phaleti rasamādāya, evaṃ gāme munī care*)."[31]

8

Buddhist Polity

In talking about social philosophy, the Buddha was aware of social realities. He always emphasized the interdependence of mind and matter, and therefore maintained that the physical or economic structure of a society affects the social behavior of people. In the *Cakkavattisīhanāda Sutta*,[1] the Buddha states that vice breeds in society owing to poverty, and poverty is due to the maldistribution of economic goods. This *Sutta* relates, in the form of a legend, how a king of the past provided all ward and protection to his subjects but failed to provide wealth (*dhana*), that is to say, economic security, to the needy for their subsistence and maintenance, and how on account of that, poverty as a social phenomenon became prevalent. Poverty drove individuals to theft and misappropriation because they needed to make a living. Therefore, the Buddha maintains that evils in the economic structure should be ameliorated if a moral society is to be born. An episode from Buddhist literature might illustrate the point here. Once a man came to listen to the Buddha's preaching and, as he looked tired, the Buddha asked his disciples to give him food and told the man to listen to his teachings after eating the meal.

In many places, the Buddha has spoken of the basic politico-economic concepts that are necessary for the satisfactory structuring of society. As we saw above, Buddhism favors the idea of the ruler being elected by consensus (*mahāsammata*) rather than being self-elected. The functions and qualities attributed to him and his kingdom manifestly show that in spirit, the Buddha desired a form of government in which the citizens' wishes are consulted and respected and where the national wealth is distributed on an equitable basis as far as possible. The ideal monarch will never rest happy until all the subjects in his kingdom are securely settled and content with their economic provisions and livelihood. The Buddha openly condemns the leader who selfishly sits on the throne, yielding to indulgence in sense pleasures and drunkeness with the intoxication of authority (*issariyamadamatta*).[2] It is said that subsistence is essential for social security.[3] If there is poverty in his kingdom, the king or the ruler is held responsible for it and it is his primary duty to see that his subjects receive basic economic needs.

Proper Leadership

A ruler should see that all his subjects are well-maintained and give provisions to those who are not. A retiring monarch advises his son and heir to the throne: "Dear son, whosoever in thy kingdom are the 'have-nots', to them let wealth be given."[4] An individual may righteously (*dhammena*) earn wealth and use it righteously, sharing it with others,[5] but hoarding up food and wealth is condemned[6] as strongly as the squandering of money.[7] The moral evils arising from a greedy disposition towards wealth or property are specially mentioned; such greed leads to avarice and wickedness.[8] A significant feature to be noted here is that the Buddha appeals to moral principles like loving-kindness and compassion for fellow human beings and to the moral consequences of anti-social behavior such as avarice and wickedness, in order to encourage men not to hoard but to share their wealth with others, and to be moderate and content with one's share. All these admonitions were aimed at the ideal of the equitable distribution of the economic wealth of the community. The reason for such moral exhortations aimed at individuals was that the Buddha regarded the society as composed of psychological units—individuals—and he believed that if an enduring change in society is to occur, it should start with a moral transformation of the basic units of the society.

In the early Buddhist literature it was thought proper to tax the prosperous provinces heavily so that some of their wealth could be distributed among the poor and the needy. This idea is illustrated by a story about a king called Seri.[9] Here the Buddha seems to approve the idea that the ruler could justifiablly tax or take from the abundance of the rich and give to the poor and the needy. Distribution of wealth to the needy is the first of the four bases of popular service of a king, the other three being kindly speech, sagacious conduct and feeling for the common good. The organized distribution of wealth (*dāna saṃvibhāga*)[10] is typical of the financial aspect of the Buddhist ruler's policy, and amounts in practice to an equitable (*sama*) distribution of wealth (*dhana saṃvibhāga*)[11] in his domain.

The Buddha maintained that the ideal type of economic distribution was the communal ownership of property, and the ideal type of political institution was the democratic system of government. But, unfortunately, he believed that both these were too idealistic for the common man, because both presuposed the necessity of the existence of a highly spiritually and intellectually developed society where greed, hatred and ignorance do not exist. Communal ownership presupposes a society of ego-less individuals. This egolessness cannot be so easily attained because those three defilements are too much embedded in the human psyche.[12] Therefore if one wants to see the birth of a equitable society, its progress must be coupled with a parallel progress in morality and spirituality. Democracy also needs a society which is highly intelligent, not swayed by emotional likes and dislikes. Actually, the Buddha succeeded in practically realizing the truth of this possibility when he established the Order of Monks (*saṅgha*) which is completely equitable in economic distribution and democratic in political constitution.[12] He recommended the *Saṅgha* as the best medium to practice and progress in morality and spirituality because it supplied the ideal socio-economic milieu for such progress.

Leadership Qualities

Therefore, for the society of the ordinary man, the best form of government was considered rule by a righteous leader. He should respect and practice the ten leadership qualities called *Dasarāja Dhamma*: generosity (*dāna*), morality (*sīla*), liberality (*pariccāga*), straightness (*ajjava*), gentleness (*maddava*), self- restraint (*tapa*), non-anger (*akkodha*), non-injury (*avihiṃsā*), forbearance (*khanti*) and non-opposition (*avirodhana*).[14]

While the concept of *Mahāsammata* was used to describe the nature of the origin of kingship, to explain the ideal ruler, the Buddha uses the concept of the universal ruler called *Cakkavatti*, in the sense that he is able to win over the whole world by the sheer power of his morality and spirituality, or in the sense that his principles of polity are universally applicable. The noble duty of the universal monarch is summed up by a retiring monarch to his son: "This, dear son, that thou, learning on the Norm [*Dhamma*: the Law of truth and righteousness], honoring, respecting and revering it, doing homage to it, hallowing it, being thyself a Norm-banner, a Norm-signal, having the Norm as thy master, shouldst provide the right watch, ward, and protection for thine own folk, for the army, for the nobles, for vassals, for Brahamins, and householders, for town and country dwellers, for the religious world, and for beasts and birds. Throughout thy kingdom let no wrongdoing prevail. And whosoever in thy kingdom is poor, to him let wealth be given."[15]

As one can see, this short paragraph sums up the whole Buddhist theory of politics. Two observations can be made about this paragraph. One is the importance it attaches to the 'right watch, ward and protection' for beasts and birds, thus emphasizing our relationship and duties towards other beings. The other interesting observation about this description is its extreme brevity. It may have been brief for an important reason, because the Buddha maintains that if a ruler respects the *Dhamma* and acts according to it, then everything in his kingdom will be in perfect order. Buddhism believes that morality or *Dhamma* is a universal power or a force that works for the benefit of the beings who follow it, as illustrated by the oft-quoted saying of the Buddha, "*Dhamma* indeed protects the person who follows it" (*Dhammo have rakkhati dhammacārī*). This moral principle permeates the whole universe and anyone who gets in tune with, or conforms to, this principle of universal morality can contact the rest of nature, because, as said before, morality is the nature of nature. Here we must remember, as will be seen in detail later, that for the Buddhists, nature is nothing other than Nirvana itself. As the principle in the *Aggañña Sutta* illustrates, there is a close relationship between human morality and nature. Buddhism clearly maintains that when society becomes immoral, nature reacts in a bad way. When society becomes moral, nature responds well: it rains on time, orders the behavior of seasons well, and such.

Therefore, the centrally important figure in Buddhist polity is the ruler who has the correct moral perspective, the 'good will' or the kind, enlightened and paternalistically caring attitude towards his subjects. In other words, the ruler's attitude towards subjects must be similar to the attitude of a mother towards her one and only child. Therefore, Buddhism does not believe in a strict political or economic theory. A Buddhist '*Arthaśāstra*' (theory of economics) would therefore be a misnomer. Once basic human values are forgotten, such theoretical structures lose any meaning or substance, and only exist as a facade for intellectual gratification. Political constitutions become mere theoretical and rhetorical verbiage to cover up human weaknesses. Economic theories end up being mere theoretical excuses for economic and social evils. Viewed from such a perspective, all discussions in political and economic theory would look like sheer politico-economic casuistry. What is important is the spirit, not the law. Once the spirit is there, the perfect laws will come into being. Therefore, a mother, or for that matter, a Buddhist ruler, need not know either political science or economics to know how he or she should look after his or her one and only child.

9

The Perfect Society

The *Saṅgha* (the community of monks) represents the perfect society envisaged in early Buddhism. The code of behavior of monks (*vinaya*) represents the ideal behavior of human beings. 'Restraint' is the key word here and a monk must conform to 227 basic rules contained in the *Pātimokkha*, in addition to numerous other rules scattered throughout the *Vinaya* collection. In the following discussion, I am very much indebted to Gokuldas De for his perceptive analysis of the early *saṅgha* community.[1]

Buddhist precepts fall into two groups: 'natural' precepts (*pakati sīla*) and 'formulated' rules (*paññatti sīla*). The five natural precepts are obligatory for laity and monks alike. They require abstention from 1) killing; 2) stealing; 3) adultery; 4) lying, and 5) taking intoxicants. The formulated precepts are for training in spirituality. Those laymen who wish to progress spiritually can observe, for temporary periods (like full-moon days), three further precepts. They are abstention from: 1) sitting on high and grand seats; 2) entertainments and perfumes; and 3) eating after midday. The first is for guarding against conceit and arrogance, and for the cultivation of humility and humbleness. The second is for training in concentration, and also for dis-identifying from the body, to discourage ego-feeling. (It is said that to enter the spiritual path one should realize that one is not one's body. This precept leads one towards that goal). The third is to facilitate a light physique that will be conducive to meditational practices.

When a layman enters the *Saṅgha*, he first enters as a novice monk. He observes two more precepts in addition to the above eight. The precept on abstention from entertainment and perfume is observed as two precepts, presumably for the sake of more emphasis. The last one, or the rule that distinguishes the monks' society from the lay society, is the abstention from handling money, gold and silver. It is significant to note the antipathy the Buddha has towards money. So, the prerequisite for entering the society of monks was the rejection of money. Thus, money is portrayed as the central social evil.

A monk must belong to the order for a particular period before obtaining higher ordination (*Upasampadā*) to become a full monk. He then must observe, as stated above, innumerable rules of conduct, meant to cultivate restraint in every possible form. These rules are supposed to be cultivated in spirit rather than in letter because the mere adherence to these rules was condemned as 'hanging on to vows' (*sīlabbataparāmāsa*). Therefore, they should not be taken as 'external rules', as Nirvana is the goal. The Buddha says, "Now all these rules combine together to make up the three trainings. What three? The training in supreme morality, the training in supreme collectedness and the training in supreme wisdom. Herein are combined one and all of these rules . . . Thus, O *bhikkhus*, one who partly fulfils these observances experiences attainment partially, while one fulfilling perfectly, comes to experience the complete attainment. Not barren of results, I declare, are these rules of training."[2]

Unanimity of the Order

In this society, unanimity was the rule. One of the creative and original aspectsof this society was that they met in provincial groups once every fortnight for the purpose of discussing their rules of conduct. This was called the *Uposatha* ceremony. De says,

"... the more important practical rules of the Disciple as chalked out in the *Pātimokkha* should be fully recognized and given effect to by all the members of the community who must regularly meet in the assemblies every fortnight in celebration of the *Uposatha*. It was exactly here that the originality of the religion of Sakya-Muni, later on designated as Buddhism, lay."[3]

"The motive was no doubt to make them live together in peace and harmony. The system of government obtaining in the *Saṅgha* being of a pure democratic nature, individual opinion in it carried considerable weight which in no other community was considered so highly a deciding factor for conducting business. Even when it was expressed through the minority it has its value. This made the *Saṅgha* invincible and, as such, it was destined to work wonders in the history of the Indian people not very long after its inception."[4]

It is interesting to note that in the ceremony, the senior monks were required to assemble together before the junior monks. "... it became the duty of the senior monks ... to assemble earlier than the junior ones so that the ceremony might not be delayed or prolonged ..."[5] "Now, what appears to a casual observer as very strange is the rule requiring that the questions and answers of the speaker on a particular subject must suit the standpoint and temperament of the sitting members of the assembly (*M.*V. II. 15, *para.* ii) ... When a member of the assembly wanted to accuse another member of any breach of rule he should first obtain leave of the person against whom his accusation was to be framed which must be done in words calculated not to give him the slightest offence."[6]

Complete unanimity of opinion was the rule of this society. "In the case of a '*bhikkhu*' being laid up with illness at some other place, his bodily removal to the *Uposatha* hall being dangerous to his life, the Saṅgha was asked to hold the meeting where he lay as the quorum consisted in the sitting of the full assembly and the non-attendance of even a single member, no matter under what circumstances it took place, invalidated the entire proceedings (*M.*V. II. 5)."[7]

Then, "the *Saṅgha* assembled for the purpose must be addressed by a venerable and competent monk in the following words: 'Let the respectable assembly hear me. Today is the 15th day of the lunar fortnight set apart for holding the *Uposatha*. If the *Saṅgha* deems it fit, let it observe the *Uposatha* and recite the *Pātimokkha*.

In the first place, let the *Saṅgha* make sure that the purity of its individual members is well maintained and guarded.

"I am going to recite the *Pātimokkha* which all of us present here must attentively hear and remember. If any one is guilty of any of the offences he must confess it; if not, let him remain silent and in this way the purity of the venerable members will be ascertained. The recital will be made three times and will be regarded as if it were addressed to the members individually. If any member willfully conceals his offence, then his action will amount to a deliberate utterance of falsehood, which has been denounced in various ways by the Blessed One as a hindrance to the realisation of Nibbana. Therefore, *Bhikkhus*, with an eye to keeping yourselves pure, you must be frank in regard to your omission and commission."[8]

De comments: "This idea of democracy in its perfection and the manner in which it was carried into operation can hardly be excelled. Even it might seem utopian and impracticable. Every individual of the *Saṅgha* had his rightful place in this system wherein his 'yea' or 'nay' was sufficient to lead the whole body of *Bhikkhus* to any direction good, bad or indifferent and might even paralyze its activities. Such a Code of laws could be worked only by the *Bhikkhus* of equal minds and saintly character with full knowledge of their responsibilities and duties and therefore it might be looked upon as belonging to the earlier phase of the constitution under the direct lead of the Buddha."[9] "The rules of the *Saṅgha* in the *Vinaya Mahā Vagga* dealing . . . with the '*Chanda*' (vote) even of the sick monk and his declaration of *Pārisuddhi* (purity) required for validating the enactments of the *Uposatha* (*M*.V. II. 1-23) may be conveniently looked upon as belonging to an early date when these monks spiritually advanced were fully alive to their duties being of the same mind."[10]

However, gradually, unanimity gives way to majority control. It is significant that Buddhism regards democracy by majority control as an inferior form of government. Thus Buddhism regards democracy as a deterioration of the ideal social form. As the community of *Saṅgha* evolved, this was what happened. "In a spirit of democracy, therefore, which dominated the minds of the [monks] new *Uposatha* rules were enacted in modification of the older ones making them as consistent as possible with the ideal of unity in purity which the *Saṅgha* held aloft before the world, although, on a closer inspection they seem to betray a desire on the part of their framers to maintain its unity rather than its purity. These rules can justly be looked upon as ushering in a period of majority control in the whole history of the Buddhist *Saṅgha*, marking the time of its ascendency in popular faith and esteem."[11]

However, it is interesting to note that the majority was not all-powerful. As De says, "under all circumstances the majority were blamable according to the magnitude of the wickedness of their purposes . . ."[12] And also, the neglect of the minority was declared a violation of law and an offense.[13]

Rules of Conduct

The rules of conduct had a gradation of significance. When the major rules were broken, like relationships involving sexual intercourse, a monk was called 'defeated' (*pārājikā*) and was required to leave the order immediately or was expelled. For other less major offenses, like ejaculation without intercourse, the monks were rehabilitated by segregating them from the community of monks for a particular period of time. The minor offenses were remedied by confession to another monk, made as soon as was possible. Otherwise, further offenses were incurred according the number of days elapsed before the confession.

The Buddha even went into minute details about etiquette for monks, and it was an offense to neglect conforming to them. Some of the rules are interesting: "I shall not eat making a '*capu capu*' sound . . . I shall not drink making a '*suru suru*' sound . . . I shall not eat licking the hand . . . I shall not eat licking the lips . . . I shall not speak with the mouth full . . . I shall not open the mouth till the mouthful is brought to it . . . I shall not make up an extra-large mouthful . . . I shall not look enviously at another's bowl . . . I shall not hide sauces and curries with rice out of desire to get more . . ."[14]

Monks were forbidden to have any private property except basic minimums like the bowl and robes. Any other property they had belonged to the *Saṅgha* as a whole. When a layman gave gifts to a monk he declared that he was giving it to the entire *Saṅgha*. The Buddha once said that it was more meritorious to give a gift to the

Saṅgha than giving it to the Buddha himself and therefore he called the *Saṅgha* "the greatest field of merit (*puññakkhettaṃ anuttaraṃ*)".

The rules for monks should be taken as description of the ideal society. What is important is to get the spirit of the rules rather than the letter. For example, as harming vegetation is forbidden for monks, one could ask how they would make a living if laymen were not there. Here, if there is no lay society, monks would have to think of practicing agriculture in a way that would involve the least violence to nature. The abstention from sex represents the ideal of complete independence, and so it should be interpreted in that sense. However, the society of *Saṅgha* could be interestingly contrasted with the later Buddhist Tantric attitude towards the world.

Duties of a Resident Monk towards a Visitor

The following account summarized by De will give an idea of the nature of the social relationships that existed in this society:

"The visitor monk was never recognized in the Buddhist monastery as a guest however distant might be the place from which he came . . . He was only recognized as an incoming member of the *Saṅgha* itself. His rights and privileges were practically the same as those of the resident monks who were therefore relieved of a great burden of formalities to be observed in special honour of visitors. Those that were observed were only just sufficient for maintaining a corporate life which the *Bhikkhus* were expected to keep up. These were: The resident monk should receive the visitor monk with courtesy and take him to the place of rest fixed for the visitors. He should enlighten him as to whether such place was being used or had remained unused for a long time . . . He should also bring to his notice matters relating to (1) families receiving education in the *Vihāra* [temple], (2) positions of *Vihāra* urinals and privies, (3) the manner in which the *Vihāra* was guarded, (4) the place where food and drinking water were available, and (5) any understanding to which the members might have come with reference to the time of departing from and entering the monastery.

"On seeing a visitor monk senior in age, the resident monk must prepare a seat for him, keep water ready for washing his feet, also provide a footstool and a napkin for his use. The resident monk should rise to receive the visitor on his arrival at the *Vihāra*, and after saluting him, take from his hands his robes and bowl and enquire whether he required drinking water. He should then remove the dirt from his sandals by a piece of cloth . . .

"If the visitor monk was a junior then he should be asked by the resident monk to place his robes and bowl at their proper places and take his seat in a room . . ."[15]

Duties of a Monk When Entering a Monastery

"The visitor monk when entering a monastery must take off his sandals and after beating off the dust from them, must carry them low in his hands. He should expose his head by closing his umbrella, and putting his upper robe on one shoulder, he should slowly walk into the monastery compound. When walking over the compound he should carefully mark the place constantly used by the residents thereof coming out or going in, be it the service hall or the pavillion or the foot of a tree. There he should go and lay down his robes and bowls and wait, taking a seat befitting his rank. On meeting somebody, he should learn from him where drinking water and food were available, and going thereto should partake of them if necessary. Before taking his food, he should wash his feet by pouring water on them with one hand and cleansing them with the other. The same hand should not be used for both pouring water and cleansing the feet. If he was a junior monk, he should clean his sandals himself by rubbing a dry piece of cloth against them or he should do it with the help of a piece of moistened cloth. The piece of cloth should then be properly washed and laid on one side. If he was a senior monk, he should cause his sandals to be cleansed by a junior monk in the way as mentioned above.

"The visitor monk should salute the resident monk if the latter was senior in age, but, if he was a junior, the visitor monk should cause the resident to salute to him. He should then learn from the resident monk which were the rooms of the monastery meant for the guests to live in and whether such rooms were being used or closed for a long time. He should . . . mark the positions of the latrines and urinals . . . When entering a room uninhabited for a long time, he should wait for a moment after knocking at the door without opening it . . . If the room was dirty and the cots were found placed one upon another or if he found the stools heaped upon one another or the bedding lying in a heap all covered with dust then he should cleanse them in the same way as a pupil cleansed his teacher's room and its furniture. If there was no drinking water in the reservoir, it should be restored by him. If there was no food, he should cause it to be prepared, and if no water was found in the water-vessel, he should also fill it with water (*C.V.* Chap. viii, 1)."[16] These instances illustrate the ideal of 'one mind' the community of *Saṅgha* continually cultivated.

The monks were supposed to help the lay society to cultivate spiritual virtues and therefore the Buddha's injunction: "O monks, travel for the welfare of the multitude." During the rainy season monks were supposed to stay in the monastery and meditate and it was called *Vassā Vāsa.* De comments: "Buddhism holds also that the best place for meditation is society, full as it is with woes and cares, and that there must be a desire on the part of the meditator to do good to it. The motto of the *Bhikkhus* should be to live peacefully among people burdened with cares and woes, and to live without trouble in the midst of those afflicted with troubles . . . Good thoughts, they believed, if cultivated within evil surroundings, had the wonderful capacity of turning those surroundings into auspicious ones. The Buddha laid more stress on the life of a monk when led in a *Vihāra* situated in the neighborhood of men who being given to the enjoyments of life, were averse to religion and undergoing perpetual agony and distress, than if it had been spent in seclusion away from their haunts. The [monks] were expected to make themselves object lessons for those who could not become monks themselves. By cultivating good thoughts in meditation amidst men of the world during *Vassā Vāsa,* they would be rendering unto the society besides themselves an inestimable benefit, calculated to accomplish the uplift of humanity from its state of stupor and dejection."[17]

The responsibility of monks towards nature and even towards their few personal belongings, is characterized by a respect for detail. One's relationship to nature is direct, and therefore it should not be approached through traditions and customs (*e.g.,* one should not waste things, simply because it is the custom). When the venerable Ananda received some new robes, Udena, the king, inquired what he would do with them. Ananda said he would pass them on to other monks whose robes had worn thin. What about their robes, Udena kept pressing him. Ananda explained that when robes were worn too thin to be suitable for attire, they would be made into protective coverings; when those became old they would be made into mattress covers, then floor rugs, foot-wipers, and finally dusters. When these, too, became old, Ananda explained to the king, "having torn them into shreds, your majesty, having kneaded them with clay, we will then plaster the walls with them." "These recluses," Udena thought in amazement, "these sons of Sakya-Muni use everything in a well-organized fashion and let nothing go to waste."[18]

10

The Bodhisattva Ideal

The Bodhisattva concept is the ultimate fruition of Buddhist ethics. It is the *Jātaka* book, rather than the other highly doctrinal texts, that has affected and shaped the lives of the Buddhist villagers for centuries. Lama Anagarika Govinda writes: "The *Jātakas* are the divine song of the Bodhisattva ideal in a form which speaks directly to the human heart and which, therefore, is not only understandable to the wise but even to the simplest mind. Only the all-too-clever will smile at them indulgently. Up to the present day the *Jātakas* have not lost their human appeal and continue to exert a deep influence upon the religious life in all Buddhist countries. In Ceylon, Burma, Siam and Cambodia, crowds of people listen with rapt attention for hours when Bhikkhus, during the full-moon nights, recite the stories of the Buddha's former lives. And even in Tibet, I have seen tears in the eyes of sturdy caravan men, when, sitting around the camp-fire, the Bodhisattva's suffering and sacrifices were retold. For these people, the *Jātakas* are not literature or 'folklore', but something that happens in their very presence and profoundly affects their own life, something that moves them to the core of their being, because it isever-present reality to them."[1]

Bodhisattva and Arahant

A difference between Theravada and Mahayana is that for the former, there was only one Bodhisattva, and that was the Buddha in his former lives, and they say that all others should aspire for *Arahanthood* or attaining enlightenment as a disciple of the Buddha, as the former ideal is too arduous for ordinary men. But Mahayanists insist that the *Arahant* ideal is still an inferior stage of perfection, because there is the possibility of further progress to Buddhahood. Therefore they maintain that all beings should aspire for the ultimate perfect state, Buddhahood. In this way, one can say that, in this concept, the Mahayana shows a definite development over the Theravada. Also, one can say that the Bodhisattva concept is the most logical Buddhist ideal which conforms to the principles expounded by the Buddha himself in the *Kālāma Sutta*, where he says that no one should follow another but everyone should try to attain one's own perfection without depending on another.

The other distinguishing feature of this ideal is its infinite commitment to others. An *Arahant* is supposed to enter Nirvana soon after death, because for him Samsara is suffering, evil and bad. But the Bodhisattva undergoes this suffering willingly in order to help others and therefore he performs the unique feat of voluntarily coming back to Samsara again and again, thus willingly postponing his final entering into Nirvana. In this sense, the Mahayanists accuse the Theravadins of pursuing a selfish ideal of attaining personal liberation without concern about others. Therefore, they say that the Theravadins have developed wisdom but not compassion, and consequently the Theravada spiritual perspective is lopsided. The Bodhisattva ideal represents an extremely subtle and sophisticated combination of wisdom and compassion.

The Bodhisattva path consists of three main stages: (1) preliminary devotional practices; (2) generation of the thought of enlightenment, and (3) the practice of moral perfections (*pāramitā*). In the first stage, one starts with doing obeisance and paying homage to the

Buddha and taking refuge in the Buddha, *Dhamma*, and *Saṅgha.*

Confession of sins (*pāpadesanā*) assumes an important place in the Bodhisattva path and therefore he confesses his sins to the Buddhas and Bodhisattvas and begs for their help and protection. Śāntideva in his *Bodhicaryāvatāra* explains the process of confession: "Whatever wrong I have done to the three Jewels, or to my mother and father, or to praiseworthy teachers, by abuse of deed, speech or thought; by many dark offences, by the evil wrought by me, Lords, whatever violent evil was done—all that I confess. . . . When one is seized by the envoys of death (*yama*), what value is a relative? what is a friend? At that moment, merit is the only protection, and that was never attended to by me. . . . Trembling with fear, I give myself to . . . the Lord Avalokita, who is entirely occupied with the practice of compassion, I, who am terrified, cry aloud a cry of suffering, 'May he protect me, a sinner.' . . . I confess it all, standing in the presence of the Lords, fearing sorrow, and with folded hands prostrating myself again and again. May the Leaders accept my sin and transgression! That which was not good, Lords, will not be done again by me."[2] After this, he rejoices in the merits of others, and Sangharakshita says that this is similar to the meditation on Sympathetic Joy (*muditā*).[3] Then he appeals by prayer and supplication "to the enlightened ones not to withdraw into the absolute quiescence of a purely transcendental state of individual emancipation, but to remain out of compassion the ever-lastingly active saviours of mankind."[4] At the end of the first stage, he transfers all the merits he has accrued, by performing the above practices, to all beings in the universe (*pariṇāmanā*) and surrenders himself to all beings (*ātmabhāvādiparityāgah*).

Bodhisattva and Self Surrender

This self-surrender is a central point in the Bodhisattva path and the spirit of this surrender is vividly portrayed by Śāntideva: "May I be an imperishable treasury for needy beings. May I stand in their presence in order to do what is beneficial in every possible way. I sacrifice indifferently my bodies, pleasures, and goodness, where the three ways cross [past, present and future], for the complete fulfillment of the welfare of all beings. The abandonment of all is Nirvana, and my mind seeks Nirvana. If all is to be sacrificed by me, it is best that it be given to beings. I deliver this body to the pleasures of all creatures. May they strike! May they revile! May they cover it constantly with refuse! May they play with my body! May they laugh! And may they be amused! I have given my body to them. What do I care about its misfortune? May they do whatever deeds bring pleasure to them, but let there never be any misfortune because of having relied on me. . . . Those who wrong me, and those who accuse me falsely, and those who mock, and others: May they all be sharers in Enlightenment. I would be a protector for those without protection, a leader for those who journey, and a boat, a bridge, a passage for those desiring the further shore. For all creatures, I would be a lantern for those desiring a lantern, I would be a bed for those desiring a bed, I would be a slave for those desiring a slave."[5]

In any situation a Bodhisattva confronts, he must always think 'what can I do, or give, to help someone in need here and now?' This thought should work as a 'moral meditation' and should be in the back of one's mind all the time. Of utmost importance is the Bodhisattva's duty to go out of his way and think carefully of the party he is confronted with, and the best possible need that he can meet. The secret here is that a Bodhisattva must be always on the alert for any possible avenue to reach out and help all beings, because that is the only way to help himself. This is the essence of the doctrine of 'the transformation of oneself into others' (*parātmaparivartana*).

There is a pithy little story in Japanese Buddhist tradition that illustrates the nature of the spirit of determination in the Bodhisattva's commitment to help others. It is given in terms of the mother-child simile. Once a baby squirrel got drowned in the sea. The mother was sad that she could do nothing to save the baby. But she thought that there was one thing she could try to do and that was to empty the sea. So she started to go down to the sea and wet her tail and come to the shore to shake off the water. Without caring for her own life, she went on doing this uninterruptedly with the idea of emptying the sea gradually. Then a god saw this foolish act and told the mother that she would die before the sea was empty. Then she told him that she knew it very well, and said that she would empty the sea as much as she could now, and if and when she dies in the process, she will make a firm wish to be reborn as a being powerful enough to empty the sea and save the child.

The most momentous moment in the Bodhisattva path is the generation of the thought of enlightenment (*bodhi-citta*). As Sangharakshita says, this is the result of a coalescing of two trends of thought. The devotee first intensifies his aspiration for enlightenment by systematically reflecting on the unsatisfactoriness of Samsara. "The second trend of thought and emotion corresponds to the humanitarian sentiment in general, and to the feeling of pity in particular. It is to be stimulated by contemplating the now tragic, now sordid, spectacles of the sins and sufferings of ordinary infatuated men and women."[6] Thus the *Bodhi-citta* is a combined result of wisdom and compassion, and the *Bodhisattvabhūmi* formulates it as follows: "O, may I attain supreme and perfect Enlightenment, promote the good of all beings, and establish them in the final and complete Nirvana and in the Buddha-Knowledge."[7] In the popular tradition this is formulated as "May I attain enlightenment for the sake of all beings, and may I not enter final Nirvana until I have helped the last blade of grass to attain Nirvana." This is the vow of the Bodhisattva.

The Bodhisattva strives always to identify with others. The technique of practicing this is explained by Śāntideva: "Another's sorrow is to be destroyed by me because it is sorrow like my own sorrow. Others, also, are to be favored by me because their creaturehood is like my own creaturehood. Since a neighbor and I are equal in desiring happiness, what is the unique quality of the 'self' which requires an effort for happiness? Since both fear and sorrow are neither desirable to my neighbor nor to me, what is the unique quality of that 'self' which I protect instead of him?" And he goes on to warn the practitioner: "After having done something for the benefit of others, let there by neither excitement nor pride nor desire for subsequent merit: Let there be only thirst for the other's benefit."[8]

He explains how the identification is to be effected: "After realizing that one is full of faults and that others are oceans of virtue, one should practice the rejection of the body and the acceptance of others. The hand [with other parts] is loved as a member of the body: Why are living beings not loved as members of the universe." Then he states the principle of one of the greatest mysteries of Mahayana ethics, "the doctrine of the transformation of oneself into another" (*parātmaparivartana*): "Whoever wishes to quickly rescue himself and another, should practice the supreme mystery: the exchanging of himself and the other." He says that it is all the better if we leave this self because it is really our enemy: "Because of an excessive attachment to 'self', even the slightest fear causes fear. Who would not hate that 'self', who, like an enemy, is a carrier of fear."[9] "Not having extinguished 'self', one is not able to extinguish sorrow; just as one who has not extinguished a fire is not able to extinguish the burning."[10] And it is this self that creates desire: "Because of desire for the impossible, there is born passion and the frustration of hope; but whoever is without hope [desire] has everywhere good and ageless good fortune."[11]

Guarding One's Mind

A Bodhisattva should guard his *Bodhi-citta* with total awareness. Śāntideva says, "In order to observe a rule of life (*sikṣā*), the mind must be zealously guarded. It is not possible to observe any discipline without guarding the quivering mind. . . . If this elephant of mind is bound on all sides by the cord of mindfulness, all fear disappears and complete happiness comes. . . . Where is the leather which will be able to cover all of the earth? The earth is covered by the amount of leather in a sandal. In the same way, I am not at all able to restrain exterior powers, but if I will restrain my own mind, what matters a lack of restraint by others? . . . As one standing in the midst of a crowd carefully protects a wound, so one standing in the midst of evil persons always should protect the mind as an open would. . . Let my possessions be lost—love, respect, the life of the body. Let any other happiness be lost to me, but never [mastery of] the mind. . . . As the mind should be examined with the thought, 'where does it wander?' so one should not cast off the yoke of contemplation even for an instant.''[12]

Here, one's enemies are one's thoughts and one should look at them as follows: "My enemies—desire, hatred, and such like—are destitute of hands, feet, and so forth. They are not courageous, and they are not wise. How can I be enslaved by them? . . . The passions are not in objects, nor in the complex of the senses, nor in any intermediate place, nor elsewhere. Where are they, then?— these that torture the whole world! They are simply illusion. O heart, renounce fear! Strive for wisdom! Why do you torture yourself in hell without cause?"[13]

Śāntideva explains how the general behavior of the Bodhisattva should be: "The crane, the cat, and the thief, walk without noise and without concern. They obtain their desired result. So should the ascetic always walk. With bowed head he ought to accept the teaching of those who are able to direct others and who help without being asked. Always he ought to be the pupil of all. . . . One should discuss the virtues of others in private and repeat them with satisfaction; but when one's own praiseworthy character is mentioned, that should be considered as an appreciation of virtue in itself."[14]

Practice of Paramita

It is the generation of the *Bodhi-citta* that makes a person a Bodhisattva. In order to fulfill this vow he enters into the practice of the *Pāramitās*, the most arduous stage of the Path. The first *Pāramitā* is the Perfection of charity (*dāna*). Many things can be given, such as material things, fearlessness, education, life and limbs, merits and *Dhamma.* A Sutra preserved in Chinese translation speaks about the giving of material things as follows: "It means . . . transcending the boundaries of heaven and earth with a charity as wide as a river and as large as the sea; performing acts of generosity to all living beings; feeding the hungry; giving drink to the thirsty; clothing to those who are cold; refreshing those overcome by the heat; being ready to help the sick; whether it be carriages, horses, boats, equipment, or any kind of precious material or famous jewel, or beloved or son or kingdom—whatever it may be that you are asked to give, it means giving at once."[15] Sangharakshita says, "In the *Vessantara Jātaka,* one of the best known and most widely appreciated of all stories of the Buddha's previous births, Prince Vessantara, in fulfillment of his vow to give whatever he is asked to give, not only surrenders the palladium of his father's kingdom but even his own wife and children. Here the question of whether Vessantara had the right to dispose of his wife and children in this manner is irrelevant. The purpose of this *Jātaka* is not to assert that a man's family is a species of movable property, to be given away or sold at will; its purpose is to show that absolute non-attachment to worldly things is an integral part of the Bodhisattva Ideal. In another *Jātaka* the Bodhisattva sacrifices his body for the sake of a starving tigress who is unable to nourish her young. The *Jātaka* inculcates absolute self-abnegation. Commenting on this episode, Lama Anagarika Govinda says:

"To the modern man such a story may appear unreasonable and exaggerated . . . because he judges from a purely intellectual, *i.e.*, external, point of view, according to which the sacrifice appears to be out of proportion to its cause. The preservation or rather prolongation of the life of some wild beasts does not seem to be worth the sacrifice of a human life.

"The Buddhist, however, sees this story in quite a different light. To him it is not the factual or objective reality that matters, but the motive, the power of compassion, which caused the Bodhisattva to act in this way, irrespective of external consequences. The spiritual and symbolic meaning of this deed goes far beyond the frame of its apparent cause.

"That the lives of the tigress and her cubs are saved, is not of such fundamental importance as that the Bodhisattva experiences within himself their suffering and despair in all its terrible reality, and that he proves by his deed that there is no more difference for him between his own suffering and the suffering of others.

"In his supreme sacrifice he overcomes the illusion of his own self, and thus lays the foundation for his later Buddhahood."[16]

However, the noblest gift is the *Dhamma* and the Buddha once said that "the gift of *Dhamma* triumphs over all gifts," (*sabba dānaṃ dhamma dānaṃ jinātī*). A Chinese Sutra says, "What are bad means? When by the practice of the perfections the Bodhisattvas help others, but are content to supply them with merely material aid, without raising them from their misery or introducing them into beautitude, then they are using bad means (*anupāya*).

"*Why?* Because material help is not sufficient. Whether a dunghill be large or small, it cannot possibly be made to smell sweet by any means whatsoever. In the same way, living beings are unhappy because of their acts, because of their nature; it is impossible to make them happy by supplying them with merely material aids. The best way of helping them is to establish them in goodness.''[17]

How should a Bodhisattva give? "He should always be very courteous to the supplicants, and receive them with every mark of respect and deference. He should also be happy and joyful, when he gives away anything. This condition is important and essential. The donor should be even happier than the recipient of the gift. A Bodhisattva should not repent of his generosity after bestowing gifts on others. He should not talk of his charitable deeds. He should give quickly (*tvaritaṃ*) and with a humble heart. He should make no distinction between friends and enemies, but should give to all alike. He should give to the deserving and the undeserving, the wicked and the righteous, everywhere and at all times. But he should not lose the sense of proportion in his charity."[18]

What should be the motive in giving? As we discussed in chapter three, a Bodhisattva should give in the following manner: "Here a Bodhisattva gives a gift, and he does not apprehend a self, nor a recipient, nor a gift; also no reward of his giving. He surrenders that gift to all beings, but he apprehends neither beings nor self. He dedicates that gift to supreme enlightenment, but he does not apprehend any enlightenment. This is called the supramundane perfection of giving."[19]

Śīla Pāramitā or the Perfection of Precepts, which is the second *Pāramitā*, aims at the perfection in the practice of moral precepts of conduct that the Buddha has formulated. An important feature of this practice is that the practitioner should not think that '*he*' is becoming virtuous because of this practice and therefore should vigilantly avoid any egotistic feelings of superiority.

Kṣānti Pāramitā or the Perfection of Patience deserves special attention because *Kṣānti* brings one closer to equanimity, a feature of Nirvanic experience. Sangharakshita says *Kṣānti* "is a composite virtue. In it are blended not only patience and forbearance, the literal meanings of the term, but also love, humility, endurance, and absence of anger and of desire for retaliation and revenge."

How can, or should, one practice *Kṣānti* if one is tortured? Sangharakshita explains in terms of *Prajñāpāramitā* teachings: "*Kṣānti* is much more than mere stoical endurance of suffering. The

Bodhisattva under torture does not grit his teeth—he smiles. This fact is brought out much more clearly, and its explanation from the doctrinal point of view supplied, in a passage from the *Prajñāpāramitā* wherein the transcendental practice of Patience is expounded with reference to the story of the sage Kṣāntivādin, or 'Preacher of Patience', who was Gautama the Buddha Himself in a previous birth. Kṣāntivādin had enraged the King of Kalinga by preaching to the royal seraglio a sermon on Patience, and the king had caused him to suffer barbarous mutilation. The *Vajracchedikā* represents the Buddha as commenting on this episode and saying:

'A *Tathāgata's* perfection of Patience is really no perfection. Because, Subhuti, when the King of Kalinga cut my flesh from every limb, at that time I had no notion of a self, or of a being, or of a soul, or of a person, nor had I any notion or non-notion. Why? If, Subhuti, at that time I had had a notion of self, I would also have had a notion of ill-will at that time. If I had had a notion of a being, or a soul, or a person, then I also would have had a notion of ill-will at that time. And why? By my superknowledge I know the past five hundred births, and how I have been the *Rishi*, 'Preacher of Patience'. Then, also, I had no notion of a self, or a being, or a soul, or a person. Therefore, then, Subhuti, a Bodhisattva, a great being should, after he has got rid of all notions, raise his thought to the supreme enlightenment. Unsupported by form a thought should be produced, unsupported by sounds, smells, tastes, touchables or mind-objects a thought should be produced, unsupported by dharma a thought should be produced, unsupported by no-dharma a thought should be produced, unsupported by anything a thought should be produced. And why? What is supported has no support.'[20]

"The last tremendous sentences are of the utmost importance. The worldling's conception is stoical. He thinks that forms, sounds, smells *etc.*, are realities and constitutive of realities, whether beings or things. With the thought that his sufferings are inflicted by real beings and things he endures them as best he can and suppresses his anger. Such a practice of Kṣānti is said to be supported by form (*rūpa*) and the rest of the six *āyatanas* (sense-faculties)."[21]

Śāntideva points out the special significance of *Kṣānti*: "No evil is equal to hatred, and no austerity is equal to patience. Therefore one ought diligently to cultivate patience by a variety of means."[22]

And he goes on to say how this virtue can be practiced: "There is nothing whatsoever which is difficult after repetition: So by the repetition of moderate pain, great pain may be endured. . . . Even in sorrow the enlightened one ought not to disturb the tranquility of the mind; because he is fighting with the passions, and in warfare pain is trivial."[23] When someone wrongs you, you must think thus: "For those who are made mad by passion, and turned to self-destruction, there is only pity. How can anger arise? If the nature of fools is that which causes injury to others, a reaction of anger is no more appropriate for them than for the fire whose nature it is to burn . . . By recourse to my enemies, my great evil is destroyed through being patient. . . . That hoard—humiliation, harsh language, and disgrace—does not trouble the body. Why, O mind, are you angry because of it? . . . Pain, whether inflicted consciously or unconsciously, is assured for embodied beings. Since this pain is beheld [only] in consciousness, endure this notion of pain."[24]

One must be neutral not only towards pain but also towards pleasures. For example, one must not feel elated when one is praised: "As a child cries in pain when his sand castle is broken, so my own mind reacts at the loss of praise and fame.

"Because it is without thought, the mere sound, "He praises me,' is not an occasion of pleasure. That which causes pleasure is the thought, 'Another is pleased with me.' "[25]

Śāntideva states the whole technique of transforming an enemy into a helper or bad into good. This is known as the Buddhist art of alchemy: "Gained without effort, discovered like a treasure in my house, my enemy is to be appreciated as a helper on the path to Enlightenment. In this way, the fruit of patience has been gained by him and by me. To him the first part is to be given, because he was the first occasion of patience. If the enemy is not to be honoured because he does not intend the achievement of patience, how then can the true Dharma—a mindless cause of accomplishment—be honoured: It is said that he is intent upon harming me, but if the enemy is not honoured, as if he were a physician who sought my health, how else is there patience? Thus, contingent upon his evil intent, patience arises; and thus he is the cause of patience and he is to be honoured by me as the true doctrine itself."[26] On the other hand, one must never dislike or hate anyone because all beings are worthy of salutation as the Buddha-essence is contained in every one: "And among beings is found this excellent particle which arises from the Buddha's Dhamma. In consideration of this particle, all beings are worthy of worhsip."[27]

Going on to discuss the *Vīrya* (Vigor) *Pāramitā*, Śāntideva says, "Thus having become patient, one should become heroic (*vīrya*), for enlightenment is gained by standing strong. Without strength (*vīrya*) there is no merit, as without the wind there is no movement. What is strength? Proper effort. What is its adversary? Sloth: attachment to contemptible things, despair, self-despising."[28] It is true that there is sorrow in this life, "but this limited sorrow is productive of my complete Enlightenment. It is like the sorrow of extraction when one removes the pain of a buried arrow. All physicians bring about health by means of painful treatments; therefore, to destroy many sorrows, a trifle is to be borne."[29] In practicing vigor, "pride [a positive attitude] is to be employed in three ways: in work, in opposition to passion, and in power. The pride of work is in this knowledge: All is to be done by myself alone. This world, self-bound by passion, is not competent for the accomplishment of its own welfare. Therefore I am to do this, since, unlike *most of* mankind, I am not powerless. . . . All is to be conquered by me, I am not to be conquered by anyone—this is the pride which I shall bear, for I am a son of the Conqueror-Lion."[30] He suggests two basic methods to cultivate vigor: "Just as one immediately leaps up when a snake is in his lap, he quickly should resist the approach of sleep and of slothfulness. In the case of every single fault, having done suitable austerity, he should reflect, 'What shall I do that I may not do this again.' "[31]

The fifth *Pāramitā* is the *Dhyāna Pāramitā* or the Perfection of Meditative Techniques and Meditative absorptions. These are common both to early Buddhism and Mahayana and will be discussed later. The sixth, the *Prajñā Pāramitā* or the Perfection of Wisdom means the attainment of enlightenment or Nirvana and the nature of Nirvana will be discussed in a separate section. As the Bodhisattva doctrine developed, four more *Pāramitās* were added, but they are of secondary importance. In his career, a Bodhisattva is said to go through ten stages of spiritual development called *Bhūmi*, starting with the stage called *Pramuditā* or Joyful and ending with the stage called *Dharmameghā* or the stage pervaded by Dharma.

The Bodhisattva ideal is a unique product of Buddhist thinking. It makes the whole distinction between altruism and egoism ultimately and absolutely meaningless because it is a perfect combination of the two, based on a profound understanding of the nature of reality. After all, the Bodhisattva, after practicing all the arduous *Pāramitās,* should come to realize this plain truth as stated in the *Vajaracchedikā Prajñāpāramitā*:

"One who has set out on the career of a Bodhisattva should reflect in such a wise: 'As many beings as there are in the universe of beings comprehended under the term *beings*: egg-born, or born from a womb, or moisture-born, or miraculously born, with or without form, with perception, without perception, with neither perception nor non-perception,—as far as any conceivable universe of beings is conceived; all these I should lead to Nirvana, into the realm of Nirvana which leaves nothing behind.' But, although innumerable beings have thus been led to Nirvana, no being at all has been led to Nirvana. And why? If in a Bodhisattva the perception of a 'being' should take place he would not be called a '*Bodhi*-being.' He is not to be called a '*Bodhi*-being' in whom the perception of a being should take place or the perception of a living soul, or the perception of a person."[32]

11

The Buddhist Concept of Evil

The problem of evil is a central one for practically all religions. In religion, evil has been made meaningful in many ways. Evil is what is opposed to the accepted goal of a particular religion. In every religion this idea of evil is present in an implicit form, although only some religions have articulated evil explicitly as a separate concept. For example, before the rise of Buddhism, evil was not treated explicitly as a separate independent principle, although the idea was implicit when liberation was equated with light and its opposition with darkness.

Among Indian religions, only the rise of Buddhism brought forth the concept of evil assuming an independent form. Evil in Buddhism is referred to as *Māra* and Trevor Ling explains that the concept of *Māra* is a specially Buddhist development.[1] As E. Windisch points out, "he (*Māra*) has become the personification of evil and death of the whole Samsara, and thus a figure peculiar to Buddhism."[2] Sir Charles Eliot confirms this idea, "No sect of Hinduism personifies the powers of evil in one figure corresponding to Satan, or the Ahriman of Persia . . . Buddhism having a stronger ethical bias than Hinduism was more conscious of the existence of a Tempter, or a power that makes men sin. This power is personified, but somewhat indistinctly, as *Māra* . . . as a personality he seems to have developed entirely within the Buddhist circle, and to be unknown to general Indian mythology."[3] These writers put forward the idea that as moral notions became centered around the unified concept of the Buddha, the opposing immoral notions became centered around *Māra*, giving unity to *Māra's* being. The Buddha's enlightenment is always portrayed as a triumph over *Māra*, and the event of enlightenment itself vividlydepicted as a battle between the Buddha and *Māra*.

Concept of Māra

Although *Māra* is personified as a deity under the name *Māra Devaputta*, the term has a more diffused kind of meaning. Therefore, in addition to the *Devaputta Māra* three other kinds of *Māras* are mentioned: *Maccu Māra* or *Māra* as death, *Kilesa Māra* or *Māra* as defilements and *Khanda Māra* or *Māra* as constituents of personality. These three kinds of *Māras* are sometimes mentioned as working under the sovereignty of the deity *Māra*. The Buddha emphasized the existential sense and significance of *Māra*, using these three kinds of *Māra*. In talking of *Māra's* domain, the Buddha explains how one existentially encounters *Māra*, in terms of *Khanda Māra*: "What is this *Māra*? Form is *Māra*. With regard to this *Māra* you should overcome your longing. Feeling is *Māra* . . . Perception is *Māra* . . . Mental dispositions are *Māra* . . . Consciousness is *Māra* . . . With regard to this *Māra* you should overcome your longing."[4] Another significant activity that makes one bound to *Māra* is '*imagining*' (*maññamāna*). The Buddha says, "One who imagines is bound to *Māra*, and who does not imagine is released."[5] In another classification, *Māra* is explained as the six faculties (eye, ear, nose, tongue, body and mind), as the six objective elements (the seen, the heard, *etc.*), and as the six kinds of consciousness (eye-consciousness, *etc.*).[6] These classifications show that all the personality factors that constitute one's phenomenal self or ego belongs to the domain of *Māra*. *Māra* is equipped with a group of strong forces. His forces are: desire (*kāma*), aversion (*arati*), hunger and thirst (*khuppipāsā*), craving (*taṇhā*), sloth and torpor (*thīnamiddha*), fear (*abhiru*), doubt (*vicikicchā*), self-will and stubbornness (*makkha thamba*), gains, favors, flattery, ill-gained honors, exalting oneself and despising others.[7] In one place the Buddha says that *Māra* has access to people by means of whatever things in the world they cling to.[8]

Māra's domain is expressed through the mouth of *Māra* himself as follows: "Mine, recluse, is the eye, mine are material shapes, mine is the field of visual consciousness. Where can you go, recluse, to escape from me? Precisely mine, recluse, are the ear, sounds, the field of auditory consciousness; the body, touches, the field of tactile consciousness; precisely mine, recluse, is the mind, mine are the mental states, mine is the field of mental consciousness." Although the Buddha concedes all this to *Māra*, he goes on to say, "Precisely yours, *Māra*, is all this. But where there is none of this there is no coming in for you."[9] Here it is interesting to note that mind and thoughts are also said to belong to *Māra*. According to Indian religions, mind is matter. Its only difference from gross objects is that it is constituted by the most subtle kind of matter, being simply another sense-organ like the eye. The ultimate spiritual principle, according to the Buddha, is *Sati* or awareness. Therefore, *Māra* can be defeated or vanquished only by awareness. This awareness leads to the recognition of *Māra*. The Buddha is unassailable by *Māra* because the Buddha recognizes *Māra* as soon as the latter appears, and to recognize him is to deflate him. As Ling says, "*Jānāti maṃ Bhagavā, jānāti maṃ Sugato!*" is the constantly repeated dismal refrain of *Māra* in his encounters with the Buddha: 'The Lord knows me! The Righteous One knows me!' "[10] This principle of the recogntion of *Māra* is vividly applied to one's thoughts. When disturbing thoughts come up, they should be recognized as manifestations of *Māra*. The three fundamental evil roots in Buddhism, *Lobha* (craving or liking), *Dosa* (hatred or disliking) and *Moha* (ignorance) are said to be the bonds of *Māra* (*Mārabandhana*). These are referred to as *Kilesa Māra*. The antidote to all these manifestations of *Māra* is said to be the recognition of them as aspects of *Māra*, through the establishment of awareness or *Sati*. The Buddha says that this way of vanquishing *Māra* could be verified experientially. For example, a bad or a disturbing thought will not be able to have any sway on you once you become aware of it. Therefore, whether *Māra* really exists or not, his mythology has an extremely significant existential relevance. When a meditator looks at thoughts as belonging to *Māra*, a very valuable and powerful perspective is provided through which to see thoughts as foreign and belonging to an evil power, thus facilitating the control of thoughts, through a process of detachment. The Buddha very often emphasizes that mindfulness is the best way of resisting *Māra*. Therefore, to keep oneself free from the domain of *Māra*, one must not make any identifications with personality factors. The Buddha says, 'Keep to your own pastures, brethren, walk on your native haunts. If you thus walk in them then *Māra* will find no landing place, no basis of attack."[11] One's proper range is explained as the realm of the four applications of mindfulness (*cattāro satipaṭṭhānā*).[12]

Ling says, "*Māra* is the mythological symbol to which may be conveniently related various factors of the human situation: the contingent ills of life and the source of those ills are, in the teaching concerning *Māra*, brought into correlation with one another in a single conception; in the light of this it is possible to discern what kind of action will lead to the transcending of life's ills."[13] "*Māra*. . . is an image or symbol of a very unusual kind, . . . and the *Māra* image is the outcome of a radical religious insight. '*Yakkahas*' (devils) and '*pisācas*' (Evil-spirits) belong to the naturalistic thought, and such conceptions appear to have risen spontaneously among men everywhere. *Māra* is not a natural feature of popular thought in this way; he is more properly to be regarded as a '*revelation*,' a conception due to the insight (*abhiññā*) of the Buddha, for without this insight, there is no knowledge of *Māra*."[14]

Thus in general, one can say that the Buddhist definition of evil is whatever it is that is opposed to Nirvana. The three basic features of Nirvana are liberality (*cāga*), loving kindness (*mettā*) and wisdom (*paññā*). So, evil will be characterized by their opposites, namely, craving or liking (*lobha*), hatred or disliking (*dosa*) and ignorance (*moha*). Although the Buddha used the semi-metaphysical principle of *Māra* to explain evil, he always made evil, as well as the idea of hell, meaningful through worldly or human experience. With regard to the notion of hell, Buddhism has two conceptions. The Buddha says, "When the average ignorant person makes an assertion to the effect that there is a hell (*Pātāla*) under the ocean, he is making a statement which is false and without basis. The word hell is a term for painful bodily sensations."[15] Therefore, the Buddha maintains that the various types of hell could be made meaningful to a great extent with the help of painful experiences in this world itself. The Buddha did believe in other hells (or painful forms of existence) in other physically different realms. However, it is interesting to note that Buddhism has no conception of an everlasting hell.

The parallel question that arises here is whether *Māra* could be a person as well. As we mentioned before, Buddhism talks of a god called *Māra.* As Buddhism accepts the existence of extraterrestrial beings, this may be suggesting the possibility that there could be higher intelligences opposed to good. However, it is important to note that this god is not everlasting. Just as other gods, *Māra Devaputta* also dies after his due time. Then another *Māra Devaputta* comes into being and plays the role. This shows that the principle of evil is an independent impersonal principle, although successive *Māra Devaputtas* become the guardians of it. Another feature to be noted here is that by being the guardians of the evil-principle the *Māra Devaputtas* themselves accumulate bad karma.

Evil is a central problem for the theist. In contrast, Buddhism starts with evil or suffering as the first noble truth. The basic ignorance, according to Buddhism, is the inability to understand that the world is evil (*Dukkha*) or non-satisfying. The nature of Samsara is non-satisfaction and the realization of the existence of this evil is regarded as the first noble truth one must understand if one hopes to realize Nirvana. What Buddhism tries to explain in the process is that evil is not in the world, but ultimately in the mind. In the world, both good and bad exist as relative to each other. Therefore, one must try to transcend this relativity and attain a permanent kind of goodness.

For the Buddha, good predominates over evil. Goodness necessarily has the power and capability to defeat and conquer evil because goodness is an aspect or a part of the nature of the ultimate reality. The Buddha's major thesis is that evil should be treated as educative. Without the existence of evil, the realization of Nirvana is not possible. Nagarjuna says, "Without contacting or associating with *Samsara*, one cannot realize Nirvana" (*Saṃāraṃ anāśṛtya nirvānaṃ nādhigamyate*). The Buddha says that "one gets an inclination towards spirituality because of the existence of evil" (*dukkhūpanisā saddhā*). Therefore, evil is a neccesary ingredient of the path to Nirvana. Two types of contemplation that are supposed to lead to enlightening results are contemplation of evil and contemplation of death. (Death is regarded as *Maccu Māra.*) The central thesis behind these techniques is the basic Buddhist idea of transforming *Māra* into a spiritual teacher.

Evil as Opposed to Correct Knowledge

Although Buddhism mentions a cosmic aspect of evil, prominence has always been given to the existential and psychological aspects of evil. Therefore, the Buddha says that in eradicating evil, one must look for the root of evil, and then eradicate it. He insists that a person is by nature good and says, "This mind is pure and self-luminous in its nature, but it is stained by adventitious defilements" (*Pabhassaramidaṃ bhikkhave cittaṃ āgantukehi upakkilesehi upakkiliṭṭhaṃ*). Therefore, a person does evil, not because of wickedness, but only because of ignorance. So, the person is basically innocent. The ideal way to combat evil is to gain correct knowledge. When evil manifests itself in society, the persons involved must be made aware of their ignorance, which actually constitutes the basis of that evil.

The idea of the transformation of the bad into good assumes a central place in Mahayana and particularly in Tantric Buddhism. This is said to be the Buddhist art of alchemy or the art of transforming dirt into gold. The technique is to treat evil as a challenge, and learn from it while transforming it through the process of learning. Mahayanists emphasize that without the existence of evil there cannot be virtues. Śāntideva, in his *Bodhicaryāvatāra*, explains this process in detail. He says, for example, an enemy should not be treated as an obstacle, but really as a blessing because an enemy gives one an opportunity to cultivate patience, which is one of the highest virtues. His argument is that the virtue called patience cannot exist without an enemy. He says: "If something does not exist without something else in which its existence is discerned, the latter is its cause. How can it be called an obstacle?" "Anger is not excused by thinking that another person has created an obstacle to one's merit. There is no austerity (*tapas*) equal to patience (*kṣānti*).

Surely, now is the occasion for it." ". . . Beggars are easy to find in the world, but one who will injure is hard to find; because if no one is wronged by me, no one will wrong me." ". . . Gained without effort, discovered like a treasure in my house, my enemy is to be appreciated as a helper on the path to enlightenment." "Thus, contingent upon his evil intent, patience arises; and thus he is the cause of patience and he is to be honoured by me as the true doctrine itself."[16] Thus, according to this doctrine, all evils are transformed into one's spiritual teacher.

This transformation of evil into good is taken to its logical extreme in Buddhist Tantra. According to Tibetan Tantrism, as expounded in *The Tibetan Book of the Dead*, death is no more a *Māra* or an evil, but a great occasion to look forward to, because the book teaches that one can find a rare type of shortcut path to liberation or Nirvana at the moment of death, and the purpose of the book is to explain that technique in detail. Thereby, death, instead of becoming a *Māra*, is transformed into a Buddha. Also, it teaches that one must try to look at one's life and the world through the perspective of death. In that sense too, death becomes a spiritually liberating teacher.

Behind all these teachings lies the Buddhist doctrine of the projection of values by the mind. The ideas of good and evil are comparative value judgments made by the mind. Therefore the ideal is to look at things as they are without using the value-imposing mind, and so adopt a neutral or an equanimous perspective. One could say that there are three types of evil. Generally we talk of two types of evil, moral and physical, yet, one might speak of an aesthetic evil, too. Moral evil is basically due to ignorance, while physical evil is due to karma. Aesthetic evil, for example, ugliness or dirt, could largely be due to one's value perspectives, and is therefore epistemological. Thus, ultimately all evil depends on the grounds of one's ignorance or one's perspective.

According to the Buddhist Tantra, there is no evil in the world, but only a causally connected series of events. Evil is either karmically generated or perspectivally generated, and in either case, good and evil belong to the nature of the causally structured universe. These two, like *Ying* and *Yang*, constitute the Samsaric world of existence. It is evil that makes Samsara an exciting and a challenging experience. Once one transcends this level, one will start seeing the interrelated nature of both good and evil, because then one will see that both good and evil have their own justifications. And one will be made aware of the beauty of evil.

12

The Nature of Nirvana

Attainment of Nirvana (*Nibbāna*) is the result of enlightenment. Enlightenment is a result of morality and wisdom which are interdependent, in the sense that they check each other. Morality practiced alone can lead to involvement with other beings, as one will not have a correct view of reality as 'voidness.' Wisdom practiced alone can lead to a kind of moral or spiritual alienation from persons and things. Huang Po in his *Zen Teachings* says the persons who practice wisdom alone are reborn in Formless Brahma Worlds because they perfect only the art of 'voidness.'

The fact that morality is related to wisdom shows that the Buddhist ethical principles involve no repression of emotions. Once in ancient Sri Lanka, a monk was making his begging rounds while meditating on the nature of the human skeleton. On the way, a woman running off from her husband met this monk and smiled at him seductively. The monk, seeing her teeth, saw a skeleton and immediately became enlightened. The husband who was running looking for her, met the monk on the way and asked for information as to whether he had seen a woman going by. The monk replied composedly, "I didn't see a woman, but I saw a skeleton passing by." This is the difference between repression and enlightenment. When the monk sees the woman as she really is, there is not even a conception of woman, albeit attachment. It is oneself that makes a woman or a skeleton out of what one sees. That is how, in the Buddhist context, one becomes the creator of one's own world.

Wisdom makes a moral transformation of the character automatically. An analogy in Buddhist texts illustrates this process: Walking along on a hot day, a person sees a ripe mango fallen under a mango tree. He becomes excited and picks up the juicy fruit. As he is just about to bite into the mango with gusto, he sees a repellent worm in it and then drops the mango automatically. This is the way one drops desires in Buddhism, and the way wisdom makes one automatically moral.

What is wisdom? It is to realize the true nature of things as impermanent, no-soul and non-satisfying. Although we may have an understanding of these concepts, why don't we become realized? Here the Buddha distinguishes between two kinds of knowledge: *Ñāṇa* and *Paññā*. *Ñāṇa* is the ordinary knowledge we all have. The Buddha said that we could never attain realization through this *Ñāṇa* because this knowledge is really a form of view or a *diṭṭhi*. In the *Aṭṭhakavagga* of the *Sutta Nipāta*, the Buddha repeatedly disparages knowledge as an obstacle to *Paññā*. Knowledge, being a view, can function as a dogma, thus covering the mind with a particular framework of ideas. Knowledge is based on thoughts which are, again, based on concepts. This conceptual thinking distorts reality by projecting our preconceptions onto things and, therefore, we can never realize the true nature of things through conceptual thinking or knowledge. What is needed is a direct experiential insight into reality through *Paññā*.

The other reason for our inability to see reality is that, though we may accept these ideas by our conscious mind, our whole personality may not accept it because the unconscious mind may be militating, silently but strongly, against the conscious mind. The Buddha accepted the existence of unconscious mental tendencies when he talked about *Asampajañña mano saṃkhāra* and *anusaya* or latent tendencies.[1] Therefore, though we may realize a truth consciously, our unconscious would not agree with it because the two are often at loggerheads and on non-speaking terms with each other. This is why we have a split within our personality. Unless we achieve an integration of these two split parts or, in other words, true personality integration, our personality as a whole will not really accept the truths we can see now. To do this, one needs an enormous amount of self-discipline. The technique of this discipline is known as *Samatha Bhāvanā* or Concentration-Meditation, which is a rigorous method of attaining perfect concentration leading to personality integration. During the *Samatha* practice, the unconscious mind gradually starts emerging out of its primeval cave, and so, by seeing it openly, the conscious mind becomes familiar with it and comes to terms with it by understanding it. When there is no split within the mind, the whole personality will at once totally accept what it sees or experiences. Therefore, after the *Samatha*, one should direct one's mind to the *Vipassanā* or Insight Meditation by which one looks at the world as characterized by the three basic features. Then one will see things as they really are (*dassana)*. It is this seeing that leads to enlightenment.

Establishment of Awareness

Although there are innumerable meditational techniques expounded in Buddhist texts to suit the particular needs and temperaments of people, there is a celebrated standard meditational technique which is supposed to function both as a *Samatha* and *Vipassanā* meditation. This method is called *Satipaṭṭhāna* or "The Establishment of Awareness."[2] The basic technique here is to watch one's actions as they happen and establish one's awareness completely on one's breath, actions, feelings or thoughts, whatever may be available at a particular time. It does not matter what one is aware of, but the important thing is to be aware of whatever comes to one's attention. This awareness has to be done as thoughtlessly as possible. Therefore the ultimate stage of this awareness is to be aware of, and watch, one's thoughts, thereby gaining mastery over one's mind by stopping thoughts.

Thinking obstructs the view of reality by projecting our concepts onto it. There are two major stages in this process of thinking. The first stage is characterized by '*vitakka*,' which denotes the onset or initial application of thought, and the second stage is characterized by '*papañca*,' which refers to the consequent prolificity in ideation. Ñāñananda examines the early Buddhist formula of sense perception, "It begins on an impersonal note reminiscent of the fact of Dependent Arising (*Paṭicca-samuppāda*):

"(1) 'Because of eye and material objects, Obrethren, arises visual consciousness; the meeting of the three is sensory impingement (*phassa*), because of sensory impingement arises feeling . . .'

"The impersonal note is sustained only up to the point of '*vedanā*' [feeling]. The formula now takes a personal ending suggestive of deliberate activity.

"(2) 'What one feels, one perceives; what one perceives, one reasons about; what one reasons about, one proliferates conceptually, '*papañceti*' . . ."

The deliberate activity implied by the third person verb is seen to stop at '*papañceti*.' Now comes the most interesting stage of the process of cognition. Apparently, it is no longer a mere contingent process, nor is it an activity deliberately directed, but an inexorable subjection to an objective order of things. At this final stage of sense-perception, he who has hitherto been the subject now becomes the hapless object.

"(3) 'What one proliferates conceptually, due to that, concepts characterized by the prolific tendency assail him in regard to material shapes cognizable by the eye, belonging to the past, the future and the present. [And, auditory consciousness arises because of ear and sounds . . . olfactatory consciousness arises because of nose and smell . . . gustatory consciousness arises because of tongue and tastes . . . bodily consciousness arises because of body and touches . . . mental consciousness arises because of mind and mental objects . . . belonging to the past, the future and the present]."[3]

"Like the legendary resurrected tiger which devoured the magician who restored it to life out of its skeletal bones, the concepts and linguistic conventions overwhelm the worldling who evolved them. At the final and crucial stage of sense-perception, the concepts are, as it were, invested with an objective character. This phenomenon is brought about mainly by certain qualities inherent in the linguistic medium. As a symbolical medium, language has an essential public quality about it. This public quality has necessitated the standardization of the symbols (words) as well as of the patterns of their arrangement (grammar and logic), and these, therefore, enjoy a certain degree of stability. Thus the letter, as the smallest unit of language, was called an '*akṣara*' ('stable,' 'durable') and language itself was associated with God and eternity by the ancient Indian philosophers. Now, the vague concepts, which are already tainted with a notion of stability owing to the limitations of the sensory apparatus, become fully crystallized into concepts in the realm of ideation. Nouns, abstract nouns, adjectives, verbs and adverbs—in short, the whole repertoire of language, assumes a certain substantial character by virtue of its relative stability."[4]

Thinking is an obstacle to seeing because it obstructs or covers reality and, therefore, distorts it. The Buddha says: "In whatever egoistic terms they think (*maññati*) of an object, *ipso facto* it becomes otherwise. And herein, verily, lies its falseness, the puerile deceptive phenomenon that it is."[5]

The attainment of Nirvana is the cessation of this *papañca* process: "Who neither goes too far into the future, nor goes too far into the past, who has transcended all this conceptual proliferation; that monk quits bounds both here and hereafter even as the snake its worn-out skin."[6] "Let him completely cut off the root of concepts tinged with the prolific tendency, namely, the notion—I am the thinker'—so said the Buddha. "Whatever inward cravings there be, let him train himself to subdue them being always mindful."[7] The Buddha summarizes the above teachings aptly when he states that "one who imagines is bound to *Māra*, while the one who does not imagine is released from *Māra*."[8]

Therefore, the Buddha tells Bahiya that the ideal way is to look at things as they are, that is, without conceptual projections: "Then, Bahiya, thus must you train yourself: 'In the seen there will be just the seen; in the heard, just the heard;in the sensed, just the sensed; in the cognized, just the cognized. That is how, O Bahiya, you must train yourself. Now, when, Bahiya, in the seen there will be to you just the seen, in the heard . . . just the cognized, then Bahiya, you will have no 'thereby'; when you have no '*thereby*,' then Bahiya, you will have no 'therein'; as you, Bahiya, will have no 'therein' it follows that you will have no 'here' or 'beyond,' or 'midway-between.' That is just the end of Ill."[9]

Therefore, the Buddha says that Nirvana is to be obtained by the stoppage of consciousness (*viññāṇassa nirodhena*)[10], because through that one attains 'ego-lessness.' It is thinking that creates the ego. Therefore when we talk of the extinction of thinking here, we must understand that what is meant is that type of thinking that is related to one's self or ego. Ego appears when one relates to one's thoughts by thinking that they are 'mine' or 'me.'

When one progresses through meditational practice one acquires the ability to enter into psychic trances (*jhāna*) and later on to psychic absorptions (*samāpatti*). In this process one also attains certain supernormal powers like psychokinesis and powers of extrasensory perception like telepathy, claivoyance, clairaudience and ability to see one's previous births. The purposeful cultivation of these powers have been strongly discouraged by the Buddha as they can lead one astray from the path to enlightenment. The last stage of the path of meditation is "the extinction of sensations and feelings" (*saññāvedayita nirodha*). Again the extinction of thought is the end. It is after this stage that one realizes Nirvana through *Paññā.*

Apart from this meditational path, there is another path through the exercise of insight-wisdom, and people who attain release through that method are called *Paññā Vimutta.* As they do not practice the meditational techniques, they are not able to attain supernormal psychic powers.

Negative and Positive Expressions

Often in early Buddhism Nirvana is characterized as a negative concept and the dominant term so used is '*nirodha*' or extinction. It means the extinction of the thought processes as well as the extinction of the attachment to Samsara and therefore the end of the process of rebirth. It is the release (*mutti*) from Samsara and therefore is said to be 'the highest happiness' (*nibbānaṃ paramaṃ sukhaṃ*). This hapiness is explained by a metaphor: when a person has an itch he gets a pleasure from scratching it. But it is followed by pain. After some time, itching starts again, and one derives a pleasure by scratching it and so on. If the itch disappears completely, then he achieves a happiness that transcends the relative pleasure experiences obtained by scratching. Nirvanic experience is similar to the latter happiness.

Another important point is that this enlightenment leads to morality, because the ultimate reality or Nirvana is, by nature, a high moral state. Therefore, a saint is 'moral by nature' as distinct form the ordinary person who is moral through conditioning (*sīlavā hoti no ca sīlamayo*).

Nirvana is a timeless state (*akālika*); it has no reference to time and space because both time and space are derivatives of consciousness. As a stage attained by the cessation of consciousness, it is best described as 'just being in the present moment,' which is also called the unconditioned or eternity.

In early Buddhism positive characterizations of Nirvana are very rare. One such formulation contrasts Nirvana with Samsara. "Monks, there is a not-born, a not-become, a not-made, a non-compounded. Monks, if that unborn, not-become, not-made, non-compounded were not, there would be apparent no escape from this here that is born, become, made, compounded."[11] Thus, early Buddhism is silent about the positive nature of Nirvana. The reason for the Buddha's reluctance to speak of the positive side of Nirvana is probably that he wanted to avoid any conceptualizations or metaphysical speculations about Nirvana. Therefore, Nirvana is called *atakkāvacara* or "*gone beyond conceptual thought.*" In early Buddhism, what the Buddha teaches, in short, is to stop the conceptual thinking process and when one stops thinking, one will realize Nirvana.

Metaphysical Analysis of Mahayana Buddhism

In Mahayana literature, the positive aspects of Nirvana are developed in great detail. In this positive exposition, they develop a sophisticated structure of metaphysics. Here it is very important to distinguish between two types of metaphysics: speculative metaphysics and experiential metaphysics. Mahayana metaphysics is made meaningful necessarily in terms of experience. They hardly lead to speculative metaphysics. Their central concept is *Śūnyatā* or

Voidness, which is a synonym of Nirvana. The nature of this voidness can be best explained by discussing the Mahayana doctrine of the ontological structure of the Dharmas or things. Edward Conze notes the basic features of the Dharmas as follows.[12] All Dharmas are void by nature (*svabhāvaśūnya*). Due to the interdependence of things, each Dharma is dependent on something other than itself. Therefore Dharmas are ultimately nonexistent. Candrakīrti says, "what has no own-being, that is nonexistent. The (absolute) own-being is a negation of (pluralistic) own-being." Dharmas have a purely nominal existence. They are mere words, mere products of conventional expression (*vyavahāra*). "The Dharmas are in themselves inexpressible." "The Buddha is the same as speechless silence." Dharmas are "without marks, with one mark only, i.e. with no mark." Dharmas have never been produced, never come into existence, because they do not really exist. All Dharmas are illusory, like a mirage, magical illusion, echo, reflected image, space or a dream. As Conze says, these definitions of Dharmas are meant to clarify two things. One is that Dharmas do not exist, as foolish common people tend to think. Secondly, Buddhism admits degrees of reality. Therefore, to say that Dharmas are "unreal" is a comparative statement. A Dharma can be unreal on a higher level of experience, though real on a lower level. Conze goes on to say that the above definitions are meant not to deny the existence of Dharmas, but to devalue the Dharmas, and to stress their impermanence, relative unimportance, weakness, worthlessness, deceptiveness and insubstantiality. Deception lies in the fact that it is mistaken for what it is not. *Mādhyamikas* prove that the existence of the Dharmas is not even logically possible while the *Vijñānavādins* prove that all Dharmas are only mere creations of the mind.

The metaphysical side of Mahayana becomes clearer in their doctrines about the *Dharmakāya* and *Sambhogakāya*. Conze discusses the nature of the *Dharmakāya*, which is synonymous with the ultimate Nirvana. "The *Dharmakāya* is non-dual in at least three ways: (i), it does not not exist, because the own-being constituted by emptiness does really exist; and it does not exist because all dharmas are imaginary and non-existent; (ii), it is unconditional because it is not conditioned by karma and passions; it is not unconditioned because it has the sovereign power to manifest itself as something conditioned, and does so repeatedly (*i.e.* as the manifestation of the Buddhas); (iii), it is essentially one, because only the belief in a self introduces such divisions as self and other, this or that; it is also manifold, because, since innumerable persons reach it one after the other, worldly convention can rightly say that there are many Buddhas." The experiential aspect of this metaphysics is clearly brought out when Conze says, "While to philosophical reflection the Dharma-body must seem to be a rather abstract concept, to the Yogin it is a matter of concrete experience. 'One experiences the *Dharmakāya*, Joyful, equal to the sky, for only one instant: At the time of (1) death, (2) a faint, (3) going to sleep, (4) yawning, and (5) coitus.' "[13] The experience of the *Dharmakāya* happens in such moments because during such events the thought processes are dramatically arrested, at least for a brief period.

The *Sambhogakāya* or the Experience Body, is a transcendental realm of temporary existence through which the *Dharmakāya* contacts or experiences the world. All the Buddhas and divine Bodhisattvas who have appeared so far in this eon are now really living in that realm without passing into final Nirvana because they want to help others to achieve Nirvana. Sangharakshita says: "So fervent was the devotion of the Mahayanists, so exuberantly creative their spiritual imagination, and so intensive their artistic activity, that the spacious Mahayana heavens speedily became populated with a glorious company of transcendental beings—Buddhas, Bodhisattvas and a host of lesser divinities—every one of whom possessed his or her distinctive attributes and individual personality. So numerous, indeed, did these *Sambhogakāya* forms eventually become that the Mahayanists began to feel the need for reducing them to some kind of order. Different systems of classification were accordingly adopted by different schools, the best known and most popular being a grouping into five '*families*' over each of which a particular Buddha presided."[14] *Avalokiteśvara Bodhisattva* has become a prominent figure that has attracted the fervent devotion of most of the Mahayanists. He is both a male and a female figure, the female side often prominent in Japan where she is called *Kwannon.* Her pictures always depict her as crying, because she cannot help beings due to their karmic burdens and because they are not asking for her help. She can help only those who ask for it. One way of devoting oneself completely to her/him is to repeat, all the time, her/his mantra: *Om mani padme hum.*

Amitābha Buddha lives in the Pure Land. Persons who surrender themselves completely to him will be helped and saved by him to be reborn in the Pure Land. A prominent ritual of devotion to him is to repeat his mantra: *Namu Amida Butsu.* This shows the extent of the role the devotional path plays in Mahayana. Thus Mahayana is more comprehensive because it tries to cater to the two major aspects of human personality: knowledge and feelings. While the Mahayana path of wisdom is for those with a wisdom-oriented disposition, the path of devotion is for the feeling-oriented. The latter path could also take one to the same goal as that of wisdom, if this devotion is practiced in a proper doctrinal context like Mahayana. In devotion what is emphasized is total surrender. If one can totally surrender, one at once becomes egoless.

It is important to remember the warning Mahayana gives to Amitābha devotees: the devotee should know that the ultimate goal of this devotion to Amitābha is to realize that Amitābha is no one else other than yourself, and the Pure Land is no other land than this world itself.

Mahayana Concept of Voidness (*Śūnyatā*)

A central doctrine of the early Mahayana Sutras was the identification of *Śūnyatā* (Voidness) with *Rūpa* (form). An oft-repeated formula is, "form is voidness, and the very voidness is form; voidness does not differ from form, nor does form differ from voidness; whatever is form, that is voidness, whatever is voidness, that is form. The same is true of feelings, perceptions, impulses and consciousness."[15] This contains the most profound implication that Nirvana is Samsara and Samsara is Nirvana. Here, the early Mahayana Sutras were speaking of an ontological *Śūnyatā* because they arrived at this through an existential analysis of Dharmas into an ontological voidness.

This implication was drawn out explicitly and formulated by Nāgarjuna on a conceptual or philosophical basis and therefore he expounds a conceptual *Śūnyatā.* He maintains that the Samsaric world is a result of conceptualization (structured by concepts). But the conceptual world is a meaningless system because concepts are contradictory. He proves this by analyzing, as examples, some of the main concepts we use to talk about the world. The central concept around which the Samsaric world is built is causality. We understand and interpret this world in terms of causes and effects. In causality we speak of cause preceding the effect. But, Nāgarjuna asks, how can something become a cause unless and until there is an effect? Viewed from this perspective, actually, the effect precedes the cause. As this is a ridiculous situation, the whole concept of causality is proved to be contradictory and therefore meaningless. Nāgarjuna says that the Samsara is built on this type of conceptually relative ideas. Through this form of dialectical analysis, he completely destroys the conceptual world. The Samsara is this conceptual world, not the world that exists as it is, which is really Nirvana. Once the conceptual world is extinguished (*prapañcopaśamaṃ*), this very world will emerge as Nirvana. Thus Nāgarjuna formulates his classic doctrine of the identity of Samsara and Nirvana: "There is absolutely no difference between Samsara and Nirvana, and there is absolutely no difference between Nirvana and Samsāra."[16]

However, it should be noted that the ontological *Śūnyatā* is in the background when one is viewing this world as Nirvana through conceptual voidness, because one has to realize that Nirvana is really Voidness. But, Śāntideva comments, "By holding to the impression of the Void, it is realized that the impression of existence is nothing at all; and, afterwards, by repetition, even this is discarded. When an existence is not accepted of which it may be said that it does not exist, then, non-existence is without foundation: How again can it stand before the mind? When neither existence nor non-existence is presented again to the mind, then, through lack of any other possibility, that which is without support becomes tranquil."[17]

The Mahayana doctrine of Samsara-Nirvana identity was further developed by the Idealists or *Vijñānavādins*, Asanga and Vasubandhu, when they maintained that the Samsaric world is exactly like a dream, and that it is experientially, as well as logically, indistinguishable from a dream. Therefore, they concluded that once one stops dreaming, Nirvana, which is there in front of oneself, will become immediately evident.

The practical implications of this doctrine of identity were not clearly drawn until the emergence of Buddhist Tantra. Tantra has often been misunderstood mainly because of its confused nature and absence of a systematic philosophical strucure (which it never intended to have). Although some of Tantra is involved in occult and esoteric practices, its central philosophical thesis can be called the ultimate fruition of Buddhist thinking. Tantric Buddhists say that the basic Tantric message is too profound, or perhaps too simple, to be understood by non-spirituality-developed ordinary people. They maintain that one would be able to fully appreciate and practice Tantra only after a good mastery of Theravada and Mahayana.

Tantric Buddhist Theory

Tantric Buddhists develop only the Mahayana doctrine of identity. This Mahayana thesis existed in seed from in early Buddhism when the Buddha spoke of the "extinction of consciousness."

The central philosophical thesis of Tantrism is best formulated in the *Vimalakīrtinirdeśa Sūtra*, a major Mahayana text. It deals humorously with the Theravada distinction between the worldly life and religious life or between Samsara and Nirvana. One day when Śāriputra, one of the Buddha's chief disciples, was sitting in solitude under a tree in meditation, Vimalakīrti—a legendary Mahayana figure who is supposed to have lived during the time of the Buddha himself—visits Śāriputra and shows him the absurdity of the idea of the retreat from the world into solitude, and the latter feels quite ashamed. In Śāriputra's own words, as reported in the Sutra: "I remember one day, when I was sitting at the foot of a tree in the forest, absorbed in contemplation, the Licchavi Vimalakīrti came to the foot of the tree and said to me, "Reverend Śāriputra, this is not the way to absorb yourself in contemplation. You should absorb yourself in contemplation so that neither body nor mind appear anywhere in the triple world. You should absorb yourself in contemplation in such a way that you can manifest all ordinary behavior without foresaking cessation (*nirodha*). You should absorb yourself in contemplation in such a way that you can manifest the nature of an ordinary person without abandoning your cultivated spiritual nature. You should absorb yourself in contemplation so that the mind neither settles within nor moves without toward external forms. You should absorb yourself in contemplation in such a way that the thirty-seven aids to enlightenment are manifest without deviation toward any convictions. You should absorb yourself in contemplation in such a way that you are released in liberation without abandoning the passions that are the province of the world."[18]

The Sutra further goes on to say that Samsara is logically necessary for Nirvana. In a conversation between Vimalakīrti and Mañjusrī, the latter explains the nature of this necessity

"Then, the Licchavi Vimalakīrti said to the crown prince Mañjusrī, 'Mañjusrī, what is the 'family of the *Tathāgatas* (*Buddhas*)?'

"Mañjusrī replied, 'Noble sir, the family of the *Tathāgatas* consists of all basic egoism; of ignorance and the thirst for existence; of lust, hate, and folly; of the four misapprehensions, of the five obscurations, of the six media of sense, of the seven abodes of consciousness, of the eight false paths, of the nine causes of irritation, of the paths of the ten sins. Such is the family of the *Tathāgatas*. In short, noble sir, the sixty-two kinds of convictions [views] constitute the family of the *Tathāgatas* !'

"Vimalakīrti: Mañjusrī; with what in mind do you say so?

"Mañjusrī: Noble sir, one who stays in the fixed determination of the vision of the uncreated is not capable of conceiving the spirit of unexcelled perfect enlightenment. However, one who lives among created things, in the mines of passions, without seeing any truth, is indeed capable of conceiving the spirit of unexcelled perfect enlightenment.

"Noble sir, flowers like the blue lotus, the red lotus, the white lotus, the water lily, and the moon lily do not grow on the dry ground in the wilderness, but do grow in the swamps and mud banks. Just so, the Buddha-qualities do not grow in the living beings certainly destined for the uncreated, but do grow in those living beings who are like swamps and mud banks of passions. Likewise, as seeds do not grow in the sky but do grow in the earth, so the Buddha-qualities do not grow in those determined for the absolute but do grow in those who conceive the spirit of enlightenment, after having produced a Sumeru-like mountain of egoistic views.

"Noble sir, through these considerations one can understand that all passions constitute the family of the *Tathāgatas.* For example, noble sir, without going into the great ocean, it is impossible to find precious, priceless pearls. Likewise, without going into the ocean of passions; it is impossible to obtain the mind of omniscence."[19]

There is no dualism for a Bodhisattva, and Vimalakīrti explains what real concentration is: "he should live neither in control of his mind, nor in indulgence of his mind. Why? To live by indulging the mind is proper for fools and to live in control of the mind is proper for the disciples. Therefore the Bodhisattva should live neither in control nor in indulgence of his mind. Not living in either of the two extremes is the domain of the Bodhisattva."[20]

How a Bodhisattva's attitude towards the world should be is explained: "When you enter a town, you should keep in mind its actual voidness, yet you should proceed through it in order to develop men and women. You should enter homes as if entering the family of the Buddha. You should accept alms by not taking anything. You should see form like a man blind from birth, hear sounds as if they were echoes, smell scents as if they were winds, experience tastes without any discrimination, touch tangibles in awareness of the ultimate lack of contact in gnosis, and know things with the consciousness of an illusory creature. That which is without intrinsic substance and without imparted substance does not burn. And what does not burn will not be extinguished."[21]

How a Bodhisattva should behave is explained: "He may follow the ways of desire, yet he stays free of attachment to the enjoyments of desire. He may follow the ways of hatred, yet he feels no anger to any living being. He may follow the ways of folly, yet he is ever conscious with the wisdom of firm understanding.

"He may follow the ways of avarice, yet he gives away all internal and external things without regard even for his own life. He may follow the ways of immorality, yet, seeing the horror of even the slightest transgressions, he lives by the ascetic practices and austerities. He may follow the ways of wickedness and anger, yet he remains utterly free of malice and lives by love. He may follow the ways of laziness, yet his efforts are uninterrupted as he strives in the cultivation of roots of virtue. He may follow the ways of sensuous distraction, yet, naturally concentrated, his contemplation is not dissipated. He may follow the ways of false wisdom, yet, having reached the transcendence of wisdom, he is expert in all mundane and transcendental sciences."[22] Or, in short, "He follows the ways of the heterodox without ever becoming heterodox. He follows the ways of all the world, yet he reverses all states of existence. He follows the way of liberation without ever abandoning the progress of the world."[23]

The doctrine of Samsara-Nirvana identity is another definite development of Mahayana and Buddhist Tantra over early Buddhism and Theravada. The Theravada goal is to flee and escape from Samsara in forests and caves, seeking release in solitude. Tantra says that in ultimate reality there can never be a duality; it should necessarily be one. Therefore, they say that the Theravada position is logically unsound. If Samsara is only a mental construction, a *māyā*, the Tantrics ask, why should we be scared of our own creations or dreams? Yet the Theravadins are afraid of Samsara and therefore their method is a form of escapism, and once they go into the retreat it is, of course, easy to control one's mind simply because there are no stimulating sense data. What is necessary is to master and get out of the dream. Once we get out of the dream, we will wake up to the Nirvana which is this world itself. Therefore when Theravadins flee from this world they are really fleeing from Nirvana itself. The Tantric message is that we should wake up to the Nirvana that is all around us. We make a Samsara out of Nirvana through our conceptual projections.Tantrics maintain that the world is there for two purposes. One is to help us to attain enlightenment. As the world is, in fact, Nirvana, the means of the world can be utilized to realize Nirvana, when used in the correct way. The worldly life is full of passions and passions mean power and force. All these forces, rather than being wasted when being channeled wrongly, could be most usefully harnessed to achieve liberation. Thus for the Tantrics, the world is a challenge, and an exciting game.

The other important point the Tantrics make is that Ultimate Reality is the strongest power principle in the universe. Therefore, once you get in tune with it, all your worldly and other-worldly affairs will be completely taken care of, and looked after, by this Power. In other words, following the *Dhamma* pays off in worldly terms too. Therefore, they say that once you win the game of Samsara you win all the way.

The second reason for the existence of the world is, once enlightenment is gained, the world is there for our enjoyment as Nirvanic bliss. Here, enjoyment is made meaningful in the way children enjoy the world, *i.e.* looking at everything as absolutely new and full of excitement and enjoyment. That is why the Tantrics say, in a sense, that we must regard children as our spiritual gurus. Thus the Tantrics sacralize the world. We suffer in the world only because we are enslaved by the Samsaric currents or worldly forces. If we can master these, the very same forces become immensely enjoyable. For example, naturally, a sea wave will engulf and kill a person. But, when one understands its ways, one can easily master it and then that very same life threatening sea wave can be used for immense enjoyment, through surfing! (Here, of course, these ideas should not be taken in a simplistic sense because they are based on an extremely profound philosophy about the nature of ultimate reality). They say that if you look at the world you see that it is full of beautiful and enjoyable things. Once we are here it is a great pity to miss the enjoyments of the world, which is in fact Nirvana. Thus, in the Tantric tradition, Buddhist thinking culminates as a transcendental celebration of this world and of this life, in this very moment.

Appendix

Buddhism And the Modern World

What is the modern world? What does it look like? The best way to see how the modern world looks would be to look at it through an outsider's eye. Let us imagine a Being from Outer Space (BOS) who has attained a high spiritual development, looking at our world from a fair distance. He would see the earth covered with a thick smog which is growing thick enough to choke man and kill him in the near future. Funnily enough, the BOS sees that this smog is created by man himself. Intrigued by this ironical situation the BOS examines the earth and man carefully. The world's resources for living are strictly limited, but man is reproducing himself at a frantic rate which has led to a population explosion. Man is raping his environment which mothers him by supplying him with food, water and air. What do we know about what the BOS sees? G.R. Taylor explains, "These resources are tied together in a complex set of transactions. The air helps purify the water, the water irrigates the plants, the plants help to renew the air. We heedlessly intervene in these transactions. For instance, we cut down the forests which transpire water and oxygen, we build dams and pipelines which limit the movement of animals.

We pave the earth and build reservoirs, altering the cycle."[1] Man's worst action is that he pollutes his own environment. Technological waste matter, like noxious gases, pollutes the air. Insecticides and pesticides destroy valuable plants like diatoms which produce 75% of new oxygen, and other vegetation which is responsible for the production of the rest of the oxygen. And radiation has become a living threat to all forms of life. The crisis is dramatically apparent in many parts of the world. Food shortages are becoming acute, a fact which becomes more and more painfully evident every day. In some parts of the world such as Tokyo, air pollution is so severe that on occasion people have to actually buy pure air for breathing.[2] Taylor concludes, "It is obvious that this process cannot continue forever: When will the poison-point come? Some maintain the world could support 15 billion people. One or two have put the figure as high as 30. The earlier figure could come in the lifetime to those now living, so the question is not an academic one. It is my belief that the collapse will come considerably before this level is reached, perhaps quite soon." So, the BOS would see man digging his own grave at a frantic pace.

The BOS, though disturbed, is fascinated by this scene and so wishes to have a closer look at this intriguing creature, modern man. As he lands on earth, he happens to see a scientist working day and night in a laboratory. The BOS is perplexed as to why he is making these high explosive bombs, but soon learns that the man is making them to drop them on his own head: so the BOS discovers that modern man is spending most of his resources for a careful planning of his own destruction. Man uses these bombs to destroy wantonly his fellow beings, animals and vegetation, and to spread radiation that is ultimately harmful to his very own self. Man's capacity for conceptual abstraction has aggravated the situation. By means of modern equipment, man can kill his own species without seeing them. He only sees the statistics and the statistics do not bleed. So, nobody, except the suffering one, is worried. The atrocious savagery perpetrated in modern wars illustrate this clearly, mightily. It may be that the scientist does not consciously see that he is unconsciously planning the destruction of his own species and therefore of himself. If he quite realizes what he is actually doing he would be appalled by his actions. This is where the BOS sees man as a split personality, a non-homogenous structure. The human personality is a structure in which several men fighting with each other are desperately trying to stick together. That is why man experiences his life as a restless and painful incident. Thus the BOS sees man himself as a veritable battleground, and as a psychotic criminal, a person who works for the destruction of others and of himself.

The BOS, being appalled by this gruesome sight, wanders off to see a typical creation of modern man: a city. There what he sees is indistinguishable from a zoo.[3] People are caged in small apartments in a highly crowded environment. It is notorious that in highly crowded surroundings of zoos, animals go mad and this is exactly what the BOS sees in the city. Due to the stress of overcrowding and the accompanying strains, man has developed all sorts of psycho-neurotic diseases. Human relations have broken down and men have become complete strangers to one other.[4] Various forms of chemical pills are fighting a desperate battle to keep an artificially induced sanity from collapsing into a surrealistic madness. Thus the BOS sees the city, the village of the modern man, as both a madhouse and a zoo.

Still more perplexed by the phenomenon of man, the BOS decides to examine the working of man's mind, in detail. He sees that man is propelled by a desire to attain happiness. It is everybody's goal in life. But ironically enough, out of millions of people he sees, he does not find a single being who has attained this goal. Obviously, something has gone wrong. What is it? The BOS examines man's mental behavior minutely. He sees a man desiring and planning to buy a radio. The man thinks that he will be really happy if he has a radio. But a few days after buying it he forgets all about the radio and plans to buy a car, after which he plans to buy a house, a shop, an estate and so on and so forth. Meanwhile, he approaches his old age and dies after being too tired, having followed one object after another. His mental condition has not become at all better than what it was before buying the radio. It has only become worse, because with increasing possessions his desires too have grown and with more desires he suffers more. The BOS cannot understand why man wants to buy 1000 acres of land when the man actually needs much less for a satisfactory living. Man buys so much land for prestige and prestige is something which exists only in the mind. So, the BOS sees that man tries to attain something from the outside world that exists only in his mind. Men desire beautiful objects and run after them. The BOS discovers that beauty exists only in the minds of men. So, again, man is running after his own mind. The BOS discovers that desires depend on the unavailability of desired objects. The more difficult something is to achieve, the greater is the desire and demand for it. Man wants to attain the unavailable. But as soon as something is attained it is no longer unavailable. That is why no man is happy, the BOS finds out. It is true that people become 'happy' for short periods, but such periods, with throbbing hearts, are fundamentally irritating because they create a restless state in the mind. That is why people tend to take alcoholic drinks at such times, to alleviate the pain that accompanies such moments of happiness. This means that man can never, by definition, attain worldly happiness because worldly happiness is a contradictory concept. Even when it is attained for short periods, it does not stand the test of true happiness. Thus man is eternally unsatisfied, and he suffers.

Thus the BOS sees the modern man as frightening, gruesome, comic and sad. He flees back to his planet. It is no wonder, under these circumstances, that beings from outer space, even if they could see us, would not even dream of communicating with us.

Of course, some of the problems we have been discussing are not peculiar to modern man and have existed since the birth of the human race, but all these problems have been accentuated in modern man, due to the many pressures he faces. The problem is not merely an academic one. If humanity is to be saved from imminent destruction, some drastic action has to be taken.

What would be the Buddhist answer to modern man's predicament? The BOS could clearly see that modern man is psychotic, sadly running wild. The Buddha's teachings can have a sharp relevance to this man because the Buddha's diagnosis of man was essentially that of the BOS: All ordinary men are psychotics (*Sabbe puthujjanā ummattakā*) and the Buddha's first noble truth was that suffering or dis-satisfaction was the pervasive feature of human existence.

What would be the Buddhist solution to the problems posed in the first scene the BOS was witnessing? The Buddha would see modern man as having clearly estranged himself from mother nature and his environment. The Buddha never singled out man as the only important creature of the world. Whenever he talked about beings he always used the words '*Sattā*' or '*Bhūtā*' which included all the possible beings in the universe. He advised that "One should be infinitely compassionate to all beings, just as a mother looks after her one and only son as her own life."[5] The *Jātaka* book portrays a world where animals and human beings share a common world with a mutual understanding of each other. In their communications with each other, man is sometimes shown as a stupid creature working under the guidance of animals who act in an advisory capacity as in the story of a king who is advised by a dog, who was the Buddha himself in a previous birth, as to how to rule a country with righteousness. The king, impressed, offers the kingdom to the dog who, understandably, turns down the offer immediately.[6] The Buddha prohibits monks from harming trees and plants because "they are creatures with one sense faculty (*i.e.* touch)" and therefore "people are aware that there is life in trees."[7] He also forbids monks to dig the earth because that would harm "beings with one sense" living in earth.[8] (He did not enjoin these rules for laymen because of the practical difficulties.) This is how the Buddha advised people to show respect to all forms of life. (It should of course be noted that the Buddha did not preach an extreme form of non violence or *Ahiṃsā* as the Jainas did, because of its impracticability. In Buddhism, *Ahiṃsā* is always an ideal to which we try to approximate as far as possible.) In this instance it is remarkable to note that the Buddha showed gratitude to the Bodhi-tree, under which he attained enlightenment, by looking at it for seven days. When the Buddha was in the Parileyya forest he was fed by an elephant and a monkey. Allowing for the exaggerated anthropomorphisms of the *Jātaka* stories, the emphatic lesson they teach us is that animals are in no way inferior to men and so we have absolutely no rights over and above them. As living beings on this earth we all have equal rights to existence. However, though some may laugh at the ideas of communications between animals and men they should now have second thoughts about their cynicism because contemporary ethologists like Konrad Lorenz and Niko Tinbergen, Nobel prize winning scientists, maintain that one can easily communicate with animals if one shows enough empathy towards them.[9] Lorenz says that he can and does talk to animals as he has proved in many of his experiments. Also, he contends that animals do have systems of moral behavior sophisticated enough by all ordinary human standards.[10] Their ethological studies show that an animal, as a living being, is not, in essence, much different from an ordinary human being who apparently differs from animals only in his complicated ways of doing things.

The Buddha's teachings show a closer and a living relationship betwen man and his environment. Man is only a part of the great evolutionary process and he will not be able to survive if he does not show brotherly feelings towards his earthly partners, who in turn help man to survive. In the cosmic time scale, man is only a very recent newcomer to earth and consequently must show due respect to his senior brethren. We must not behave as hosts but only as guests on this earth. Thus Buddhism never portrays man as carrying any singular value- significance as far as living is concerned. Therefore it would be a gross mistake to call Buddhism merely humanistic. Chambers dictionary defines Humanism as "any system which puts human interests and the mind of man paramount." In this sense, Buddhism is clearly 'anti-humanistic' because it is emphatically against making man a privileged being. It is the anthropocentric pride that has made man feel that he is the owner of animals and plants and it is this very pride that will gradually choke him and cause his end.

The Buddha always praised the person who had a clear sense of proportion (*Mattaññū*). Everything has a balance and when it is reached, one must be content. It is 'balance' and 'proportion' that have become key words in the present battle against the population explosion.

We may already know or readily appreciate what we have been saying so far. But we find it equally difficult to put into practice what we appreciate so much. Why is that? It is beause we cannot help doing destructive or bad things because of certain innate characteristics that are built in us. To understand these we must analyze man a little more deeply.

Man, a result of the cosmic process of evolution, evolved from animals through processes of mutation. Therefore to understand man fully, we have to understand his ancestors. Man is basically an animal. Whether we believe in the evolutionary process or not, the simple hard fact is that the ordinary man is hardly distinguishable from an animal, in all his day-to-day activities. The only difference is that what the animal does is a simple way, man does in a much more complex manner. Though we pride ourselves as heirs to sublime ethical principles, animals have had comparable systems long before us. The simple fact is that morality is only a system of rules that has gradually evolved for safeguarding the species in the evolutionary process. The fittest survives. Morality makes a species the fittest to survive.

What are the basic needs of an animal? Robert Ardrey explains, "... in all higher animals, including man, there are basic, inborn needs for three satisfactions identity, stimulation and security. I described them in terms of their opposites: anonymity, boredom and anxiety . . . To a surprising degree, however, security ranks lowest among our needs and the more thoroughly we achieve it, the more willingly do we sacrifice it for stimulation. So long as we live in a milieu of material deprivation, the illusion that security is paramount will enclose us; and many an error of social philosophy has so been written. But let even a minimum of affluence replace deprivation's demands, and security will give away to boredom, a condition to be avoided."[11] The need for identity ranks highest. We would not mind sacrificing everything to achieve fame. It is the need to bolster up the idea of "I" or the ego. The way in which this need is accomplished in animals is that they have an innate need for a territory of their own and this provides them with security as well. One of our basic needs is that we need our own house: our own territory. It is a territorial imperative.[12] Animals have an innate relationship to their territories. We all know how a cat or a dog, left miles away from its original home, manages to find the way back. Ardrey explains how birds jet-flown from the United Kingdom to America and from Philippines to America have mysteriously managed to find their way back home. Unless they had an innate sense of their territory, how could they accomplish this type of miraculous feat? According to ethologists, there is a basic character trait that is fundamentally essential to fulfill the three basic needs and that is aggression. It is needed for survival. Lorenz says that because of aggression there results a "balanced distribution of animals of the same species over the available environment, selection of the strongest by rival fights and defense of the young."[13] Also, there is a ranking order, a hierarchical setup in most animal societies. Hierarchy makes a society of animals into a cohesive, strong organization. Without this type of ranking organization, species could not survive. Aggression is needed to secure this setup by selecting the strongest to lead the organization. It is also this type of organization that facilitates the keeping of peace within the society. Within the organization there is amity, but towards outsiders is directed enmity. This is how the amity-enmity complex arises. The whole of morality is directed, towards the preservation of a particular organization of species. Evolution wants to preserve species not individuals. That is why altruism has developed. Many people are of the opinion that altruism is exclusively a sublime moral possession of man. But this is irrefutably disproved by the findings of ethologists. In animal organizations we can see how animals 'sacrifice' their individual lives to preserve their fellow beings. Hierarchical Organizations are meant to achieve exactly this purpose. (An army illustrates this point well.) Eugene Marais, who spent most of his life with baboons, describes an event where two baboons carefully plan to kill a tiger, in the process of which they sacrifice themselves to save their group. In that context, theirs is a sacrifice in the full human sense of the term.[14] Although in some contexts we obey moral rules without any necessity, what we actually do there is to attempt to endorse a moral rule which in other normal contexts performs a valuable function to preserve the species. All good and bad and the whole of morality is meant only to serve the function of preserving the species. (There is, of course, a path to spiritual progress through morality, but this latter morality is a unviersal morality, *i.e.*, compasion and love for all beings. Ordinary morality is always a group morality, *e.g.*, communal or nationalistic. However, even universal morality is also only a steppingstone to spiritual progress.) Human societies behave exactly like societies of rats, who are friendly towards the members of their own community but mortal enemies to outside members of their own species. If our BOS was an ethologist and knew about rats, he too would conclude that human species are genetically related to rats!

Thus, aggression is a pervasive feature in all life. Psychologists say that it is innate like sex.[15] Therefore it is a spontaneous drive.[16] That means, if we do not have enemies we always tend to make them because otherwise we cannot discharge our aggression. If we carefully observe our own behavior, we can easily see how we do this ourselves. There is unity when we fight against a common enemy.

When that enemy disappears, we soon start fighting among ourselves because we just have to find objects to discharge our aggression. The Buddha always emphasized that aggressive tendencies (*dosa* and *māna*) are clearly innate in us. They exist in children in latent forms known in Pali as *Anusayas.*[17] The *Visuddhimagga* defines *dosa* as follows: "It has the characteristic of savageness, like a provoked snake. Its function is to spread, like a drop of poison, or its function is to burn up its own support, like a forest fire. It is manifested as persecuting, like an enemy who has got his chance. Its proximate cause is the grounds for annoyance. It should be regarded like stale urine mixed with poison."[18] However, ethologists have failed to emphasize an equally important drive. That is *lobha* or greed. It is the 'I' feeling or self-expansion that makes one aggressive. After obtaining our desired objects, we soon look for other objects to attain. This again shows how *lobha* is a spontaneous innate drive. The drive cannot be stopped by obtaining outside things. However many things we obtain, the *lobha* drive will be there.

How did the Buddha solve the fundamental problems of *lobha* and *dosa*? Many think that the Buddha asked us to destroy them completely. But if they are innate drives within us, can they be destroyed like that? If they are the very basic pattern of life, how can they be destroyed? It is a grave mistake to think that he asked us to do so. He never advised to leave out *taṇhā* or *lobha* completely. He only asked us to destroy that type of *taṇhā* and *dosa* that leads to the making of bombs and human suffering. He asked us to be mortal enemies of this type of *dosa* and *taṇhā* and wage a massive aggressive war against it. He himself fought this war (*Māra Yuddha*) and as he won it he was called Jina, the Winner. To do this, one must have *taṇhā* for liberation and he said that "*Taṇhā* should be destroyed by *taṇhā*." When one sees an *Arahant* one must cultivate self-conceit or *māna* thinking, """If he can attain this state why cannot I?" And thus, again, "*Māna* should be destroyed by *māna*."[19] This is the way the Buddha explained how we should sublimate our innate instincts.

How can we destroy harmful *lobha* and *dosa*? It is the asking of this question that makes man different from animal. Here man is asking how he could transcend the animal level of existence and it is the ability to ask this crucial question that makes an animal a human being. The Buddha said that to destroy *lobha* and *dosa* we must first study how they arise, and maintained that they arise from ignorance, partly of the external world and partly of ourselves. We are ignorant of the real nature of things of the external world. *Lobha* originates due to this ignorance. To illustrate, let us say we have a desire to buy a beautiful house. In the process of obtaining this end, we might have to undergo suffering, first by thinking about not possessing it at that time, then toiling to find money, undergoing various hardships and scheming to obtain it. In the course of this we might become aggressive towards some persons, leading perhaps to fights or even murders. This whole mass of worry and suffering originates because of the beautiful house. But, are houses beautiful? The BOS would see all our houses as just places of shelter. Therefore, beauty is not in the house. A beautiful house in Africa may not be beautiful in another country. The idea of beauty varies dramatically from place to place and from time to time. Beauty is only a conceptual convention in the context of a particular time and place. In other words, beauty is no more than a concept that exists only in our minds. When we see a house as beautiful, we are projecting our concepts onto objects and seeing a part of our mind in the object. We are going after our own mind when we go after beautiful objects.

Now, if beauty does not exist as such in the outside world, does the house exist there as an object? If the house is demolished part by part, what we would see is only a heap of stones and bricks. What happened to the house? Where did it go? It did not go anywhere because it did not exist, to begin with. When the parts were arranged in a particular way, we had the concept of the house. Therefore, the house existed only in our minds, as a concept.[20] If we reduce parts to their minute particles we will end up in elements (*mahābhūta*) of air, water, earth, *etc.* which are, again, only tiny heaps of evanescent changes or of energy. So, what really exists in the outside world is only energy or processes of change materializing in the form of *mahābhūta*, the latter themselves being conceptual products. They are called Great *Bhūtas* or Spirits because it is they who like spirits (or demons) create various magical things like houses to deceive us!

Let us look at the house from another angle. Physical objects exist only in relation to sense organs. If our sense organs were constituted differently we would not see the objects we normally see now. If our eyes were as sharp as electron microscopes we would see only a mass of swirling atoms, never any physical object. Likewise with regard to other sense organs. If our sense organs and mind were constituted in a radically and transcendently different manner, then we would perhaps see nothing, a compelte emptiness or voidness (*Suññatā, Animitta*). Thus the existence of physical objects depends directly on our physical constitution. So, again, this shows how we conceptualize and make objects with the help of the outside energy or processes of change, which manifest themselves to us as *mahābhūta*. If we look at the houses as they really are, *i.e.* simply as processes of change, then we would see that there is no house that is worth getting attached to. Although we would still see the house, there would not be any attachment to it. With that, the whole mass of suffering that could arise with the idea of the house disappears.

Let us illustrate the same idea with the help of a sensual pleasure. When we see an unattractive woman walking on the street, we note casually that a woman is walking on the road. But if we see a beautiful woman walking, we get excited, we think that she is an angel from heaven. We might have various sexual fantasies, and may pine for her and make plans to secure her, thereby initiating a complicated sequence of events that would lead to frustrations, anxieties and a mass of suffering. If we could see her as she really is, *i.e.*, as just another woman or a human being, then none of this self-inflicted suffering would have arisen. As we know, beauty is a notoriously relative concept, and is normally regarded as being "in the eye of the beholder." So, when we love a beautiful woman, we have projected our own concepts onto her. Therefore what we are actually doing is loving our own mind, and running after our own mind. When we secure her, she becomes available, and our mind immediately jumps on to another unavailable woman and sees her as beautiful and pines to secure her, temporarily or permanently. The Buddha says, that in such situations we are "obsessed with concepts."[21] The Buddha said that "Man's sensual desires are only attachments to concepts."[22] That is why whole processes of sensual experiences can be effectively executed in a dream, with entirely satisfactory results. If we see the beautiful woman only as a creation of our concepts and see her only as a group of *mahābhūta*, then the whole mass of suffering attendant on thinking of her as a woman disappears. This way of looking at the world has been explained in the *Mūlapariyāya Sutta* where the

Buddha says that "earth should be seen as earth, water as water" etc.[23]

The other side of the picture is the 'I'. It is 'I' who desires and suffers. Does this 'I' exist? If you look into yourself, you will never find this 'I'. The Buddha analyzed a person into five factors like form (*rūpa*), feelings (*vedanā*), *etc.*, but did not find a self or a soul in any of them. If so, how do we get this feeling of 'I'? It is an illusion, a result of conceptualization. As we conceptualize and make outside objects through projection, we get the idea of self in relation to the conceptual-world-building process. Sitting in a stationary train, if we look at a moving train, we see our train as moving.[24] Likewise, in relation to the conceptual projections we make on to the external world, we tend to see an 'I'. If we stop these conceptual projections, the 'I' will vanish instantly. The self grows by identifying itself with things. First, the self identifies itself with the body, then with other objects like one's car. The more one desires and obtains, the more the self grows. As the self grows bigger, one wants to achieve bigger and bigger things to satisfy the growing self. Therefore, as one achieves more and more possessions, one has to suffer more and more. The 'I' goes on identifying with various things until it ends up in abstract concepts, like nation, religion, *etc.* Partly, it is the fear of death and craving for immortality that propels one towards this type of identification. Nations and religions last longer than individuals. Therefore, by identifying with them one gets an illusory feeling of immortality. This is also a trick that evolution plays on individuals, so that individuals by identifying themselves with species will regard the latter as higher than one's individual life, thus facilitating the preservation of the species. We saw how this was operative among baboons. This is clearly seen operating among insects like ants in a semiconscious way.

Thus there are two ways to 'stop the world.' One is by stopping conceptualization so that it will dissolve the world and thereby the 'I'. The other is by destroying the world-building center, the 'I'. Thus when you see objects in the world, you are only seeing a screen made up of your own concepts. (Behind the screen are energies in the form of *mahābhūta.*) Funnily enough, you yourself are on this very same screen. You can go behind yourself and watch yourself on the screen watching other things. You can see yourself, on the screen, getting excited, desirous and anxious about the very things you yourself have made! This is, of course, a veritable moment for laughter and in this sense, laughter can have a great emancipatory value.

Now one can ask: "We all know this now, but why don't we attain *Nibbāna*?" Unfortunately what we have now is only knowledge. The Buddha often degraded knowledge or ñāṇa as being similar to a view or *diṭṭhi*.[25] *Ñāṇa* has to be discarded by seeing reality by *paññā* or *aññā*, which is wisdom.[26] Mere knowledge does not affect our behavior because our mind has two types of functions, conscious and unconscious, the mind being only a series of functions. The Buddha accepted the existence of unconscious mental tendencies when he talked about *Asampajjañña mano saṃkāra* and *Anusaya* or latent tendencies.[27] Therefore, though we may realize a truth consciously, our unconscious would not agree with it because they are often at loggerheads and on non-speaking terms with each other. This is why we have a split within our personality. Unless we achieve an integration of these two split parts or, in other words, a true personality integration, our personality as a whole will not really accept the truths we can see now. To do this one needs an enormous amount of self-discipline. The technique of this discipline is known as *Samatha Bhāvanā* or Concentration-Meditation, which is a rigorous method of attaining perfect concentration leading to a personality integration. Once this integration is achieved, one can direct one's mind to see "things-as-they are" (*yathābhūta dassana*) and this will result in the realization of *Nibbāna*. This is how one transcends one's animality and becomes even more than human. Western ethological thinkers are rather pessimistic that man will be able to conquer his animal nature.[28] It is here that Buddhism can be relevant in showing that there is a perfectly sensible path to transcend our animal natures. Ironically enough this transcendence is effected by exploiting or sublimating the very animal instincts that torment us. Once we attain *Nibbāna* what will happen to our sublimated *taṇhā* and *dosa*? The Buddha once explained that once you have a desire to go to a particular place, that desire will no longer be there once you have arrived at that place.[29] Once you have realized that there is no person called 'I,' your *dosa* and *māna* (conceit) will dissolve themselves automatically.

When one knows things-as-they-really-are then one knows that there are no enemies or friends, beautiful things or ugly things in the world. There are only neutral beings and neutral things in the world. Then one looks at the world with true equanimity (*Upekkhā*). These beings and objects are again only elements on one's conceptual screen that one projects onto outside processes of change or energy that exist in the world. Thus when we look at the world, we are actually looking only at our own mind. When we know the true nature of beings and objects, then we understand that they deserve neither our desire nor our hate.

Knowledge of *yathābhūta* leads to true love. When one accepts things as they are, one does not pass value judgments on them. Thus, moralization will stop. When an ideal mother looks at her only son, she looks at him "as he really is" or as "things-as-they-are," without passing any value judgments on him. That is how that unique love a mother has towards her child originates. Parents look at their sons as an *Arahant* looks at beings. That is why ideal parents have been called Brahmas by the Buddha. The Buddhist tradition says that the mother is the Buddha at home. The Buddha often took the example of a mother's love towards her son to illustrate how an *Arahant* looks at all beings in the world. It is acceptance of things as they are. Here one goes beyond morality. That is why an *Arahant* has been described as having gone beyond both good and bad.[30] He has transcended ordinary morality.

It is instructive to find that some modern psychological studies have found a technique that is very similar to the Buddhist method as effective in recovering sanity in modern society. Anthony Storr says: "An alienated person is so because through fear, guilt, self-abasement or suspicion he is unable to communicate freely with others. He cannot reveal his true self to another human being because he does not believe that any other human being can accept him as he really is."[31] He says that the most effective psycho-therapeutic technique is the loving acceptance of a patient as he really is and says, "It is love which really heals the patient."[32] Victor Frankl says that once a female patient came to him, but, after carefully listening to her for some time, he referred her to another psychotherapist because he could not understand what she was saying as she was talking in a strange accent. But she had not consulted the other doctor, he found out later. However, a few months later when he met her on the street she started thanking him profusely for curing her illness. Frankl says, up to this date he does not know what she was suffering from.[33]

Erich Fromm says that Buddhism has really mastered the principles of sane psychology and maintains that contemporary psychology has yet to learn its lessons from Buddhism if modern society is to be saved from a mass insanity.[34]

The Buddha taught that what is basically necessary is the correct perspective of looking at things, which results in love. This is the Buddhist solution to the problems of the modern world. However, one might say that Buddhism cannot be a panacea for modern problems because there are so many other problems, like economic problems. But while recognizing such problems and suggesting separate solutions for them, the Buddha would still say that the fundamental necessity is to get the correct perspective of looking at things-as-they-really-are. This would make everybody a mother. And, of course, a mother need not study economics to learn how to support her one and only child.

This appendix entitled 'Buddhism and the Modern World', was a talk given in Sinhalese as the Gunapala Malalasekara commemorative lecture in the All Ceylon Buddhist Congress, Colombo, on April 23, 1975. Its English translation appeared in Narada Felicitation Volume (Buddhist Publication Society Kandy, 1979).

Footnotes

Chapter One: Background to Buddhist Ethics

1. *A.I.* 189ff. A major secondary source for the early Buddhist theory of knowledge is, *Early Buddhist Theory of Knowledge*, by K.N. Jayatilleke.

2. *M.* I. 317.

3. *M.* I. 482.

4. *M.* I. 320.

5. *Dhp.* 97, *S.* IV. 138; *M.* II. 173.

6. *M.* I. 520.

7. *M.* I. 230.

8. *M.* II. 170-1.

9. *E.B.T.K.*, Chap IX.

10. *M.* II. 197, *A.* II. 46; *E.B.T.K.*, pp. 281ff.

11. *D.* II. 104, III. 125; *M.* II. 33.

12. *M.* III. 230, 234.

13. *E.B.T.K.*, pp. 340ff; Jayatilleke K. N., 'The Logic of Four-Alternatives,' in *Philosophy East and West*, Moore Memorial Vol-

ume, Vol. XVII, No. 1-4, pp. 78-9.

14. D. I. 83-4.

15. Malalasekara, G.P. and Jayatilleke, K.N., *Buddhism and the Race Question*, p. 32.

16. *A*. I. 227-8.

17. *A*. IV. 429.

18. *A*. IV. 138.

19. Malalasekara and Jayatilleke, p. 33; *A*. IV. 39, 40.

20. *M*. I. 486.

21. *S*. IV. 95.

22. *A*. II. 48.

23. *S*. IV. 39-40.

24. It seems that the necessary precaution has been taken in the above *Samiddhi Sutta* itself. In addition to the three factors, the eye, the visible forms and the visual consciousness, it refers to a fourth, i.e., 'things perceptible with visual consciousness.' Ñaṇananda, Bhikkhu, *Concept and Reality*, Kandy: BPS., 1971, p. 75.

25. *Ibid.*

26. Dharmasiri, Gunapala, 'Buddhism and the Modern World,' in *Narada Felicitation Volume*, Ed. Piyadassi Thera. Reprinted here as the Appendix.

Chapter Two: Motivation in Buddhist Ethics

1. *S*. pp. 13-4.

2. Jayatilleke, K. N., *Ethics in Buddhist Perspective*, P. 26; M. II. 27.

3. Cook, Francis, H., *Hua-yen Buddhism*, p. 81. About the Theravada-Mahayana controversy, see *Discerning the Buddha*, Lal Mani Joshi, Delhi: 1983, pp. 1-53.

4. *Ibid.*, p. 82.

5. *Ibid.*, pp. 82-3.

6. *M*. I. 97.

7. *M*. I. 38.

8. *Sn*. 149.

9. *S*. V. 353-4.

10. *Sn.* 146, 147.
11. *Vinaya,* IV, 34.
12. *Vinaya,* IV, 32-3.
13. *D.* I. 124.
14. *A.* V. 2.

Chapter Three: Criteria of Good & Bad

1. *A.* I. 203.
2. *Dhp.* X. 1.
3. *M.* I. 102.
4. *Vajracchedikā Prajñāpāramitā.* Tr. Edward Conze, (*Buddhist Wisdom Books*), p. 26.
5. *Ibid.*, P. 25.
6. *Ibid.*, p. 54.
7. *Pañcaviṃśatisāhaśrikā.* Tr. Edward Conze, Buddhist Texts Through the Ages, pp. 136-7.
8. Conze, *Buddhist Wisdom Books,* p. 26.
9. *Ibid.*, p. 39.
10. *Sn.* 790.
11. *Netti.* 184.
12. *M.* III. 29.
13. Jayatilleke, *Ethics.*, p. 26.
14. *Ibid.*, p. 24.
15. *M.* I. 407.
16. *A.* I. 193.
17. *S.* V. 387-8.
18. *M.* I. 180.
19. *Vsm.* 54.

Chapter Four: Karma and Rebirth

1. *A.* III. 186.,
2. Jayatilleke, *Ethics.*, p. 11.
3. A. III. 415.
4. Silva, Padmasiri de, *Buddhist and Freudian Psychology,* pp. 49-70.
5. *Dhammapadaṭṭhakathā.* 3ff.

6. *A.* I. 173-4.
7. Jayatilleke, K.N. *Survival and Karma in Buddhist Perspective, Milinda Pañha,* 40.
8. *Tibetan Book of the Dead,* Tr. Evans Wentz.
9. *M.* I. 387-392.
10. Stevenson, Ian, *Twenty Cases Suggestive of Reincarnation*; proceedings of *The American society for Psychical Research,* Vol. XXVI, September 1966.
11. Rodney, Jonathan, *Explorations of a Hypnotist.*
12. Moody, Raymond, *Life and Life.*

Chapter Five: Sublime Virtues

1. *D.* II. 251 (Eightfold path: Right understanding; Right thought; Right speech; Right action; Right livelihood; Right effort; Right mindfulness; Right concentration).
2. *M.* I. 351.
3. *A.* I. 110.
4. *A. A.* I. 70.
5. *D.* III. 237.
6. *M.* I. 206-207.
7. *Vsm.* 295; *PP.* p. 321 (i.e. *The Path of Purification,* Tr. Bhikkhu Nanamoli.)
8. *Vsm.* 297, *PP.* p. 323.
9. *Vsm.* 299-300.
10. *Vsm.* 302, *PP.* pp. 331-2.
11. *Vsm.* 305-7, *PP.* p. 331-2.
12. *A. A.* 82-3.
13. Aronson, H. *Love and Sympathy in Theravada Buddhism,* pp. 62-4.
14. *Vsm.* 317-8, *PP.* pp. 343-4.
15. Aronson, p. 63.
16. *Vsm.* 318, *PP.* pp. 343-4.
17. *Vsm.* 314-5, *PP.* p. 340.
18. Aronson, pp. 62-4.
19. *Vsm.* 318, *PP.* p. 345.
20. Aronson, pp. 64-5.

21. *Vsm.* 318, *PP.* pp. 345.
22. Aronson, p. 65.
23. *Ibid.*, pp. 65-6.
24. *Vsm.* 321, PP. p. 347.
25. Aronson, p. 6.
26. *M.* I. 392-5.
27. Aronson, p. 16.
28. *Ibid.*, p. 20.

Chapter Six: The Origin and Nature of Society

1. *D.* III. 80-98.
2. *Sn.* 144.

Chapter Seven: Buddhist Social Ethics

1. G. S. Ghurye, *Caste and Race in India*, p. 84
2. Malalasekara & Jayatilleke, p. 26.
3. *The Laws of Manu*, Tr. G Buhler, *Sacred Books of the East*, Vol. XXV, Chapter X.
4. *Ibid.*, III. 156.
5. Malalasekara & Jayatilleke, p. 27.
6. *The Law of Manu*, X. 4.
7. *Ibid.*, III. 183.
8. *Āpastambha Dharmasūtra*, II. 16, 27. As quoted by Malalaseka and Jayatilleke, pp. 26-7.
9. *The Law of Manu* , X.
10. *M.* I. 85-89.
11. *D.* III. 96.
12. *Loc. Cit.*
13. *Ibid.*, 97.
14. Malalasekara & Jayatilleke, p. 35.
15. *Ibid.*, p. 39.
16. *Ibid.*, pp. 34-5.
17. *D.* III. 181-2.
18. *D.* III. 183-4.
19. *Ibid.*, 184.

20. *Ibid.*, 186-7.
21. *Ibid.*, 188.
22. *Loc. Cit.*
23. *Ibid.*, 189.
24. *S. B. B., Dialogues of the Buddha,* Part III, Tr. Rhys Davids, p. 180, fn. 4.
25. *D.* III. 190-1.
26. *Ibid.*, 192.
27. *Sn.* p. 18ff.
28. *Sn.* p. 21ff.
29. *Sn.* p. 46ff.
30. *The Book of Protection,* Tr. Piyadassi Thera, p. 26.
31. *Dhp.* IV. 6.

Chapter Eight: Buddhist Polity

1. *D.* III. 58ff.
2. S. I. 100, Also, 'Buddhism and Marxism in the Socio-Cultural Context of Sri Lanka,' *Buddhism and Western Philosophy,* Ed. Nathan Katz, pp. 134-48.
3. *D.* III. 65.
4. *D.* III. 61.
5. *S.* IV. 336; *A.* III. 66, 68.
6. *D.* III. 90, *A.* I. 87.
7. *A.* I. 87.
8. *D.* III. 289.
9. *S.* I. 58.
10. *D.* III. 145.
11. *D.* III. 61, 65.
12. Dharmasiri, 'Buddhism and the Modern World,' pp. 94ff. See appendix.
13. De, Gokuldas, *Democracy in Early Buddhist Saṅgha.*
14. *J.* III. 274, *J.* I. 260, 399.
15. *D.* III. 61.

Chapter Nine: The Perfect Society

1. De, Gokuldas, *Democracy in Early Buddhist Saṅgha.*
2. *A.* III. 9, 86.
3. De., p. 62.

4. *Ibid.*, p. 63.
5. *Ibid.*, p. 68.
6. *Ibid.*, p. 69.
7. *Ibid.*, p. 75.
8. *Ibid.*, pp. 63-4.
9. *Ibid.*, p. 74.
10. *Ibid.*, pp. 75-6.
11. *Ibid.*, p. 76.
12. *Ibid.*
13. *Ibid.*, pp. 79ff.
14. *The Pātimokkha*, Tr, Ven. Ñāṇamoli, p. 78.
15. De., pp. 113-4.
16. *Ibid.*, pp. 112-3.
17. *Ibid.*, pp. 87-8.
18. *C. V.* 291-2.

Chapter Ten: The Bodhisattva Ideal

1. Govinda, Lama Anagarika, 'Origins of the Bodhisattva Ideal,' *Stepping Stones*, Vol. II, January 1952. p. 244.
2. Śāntideva, *Bodhicaryāvatāra*, Tr. Marion L. Matics, *Entering the Path of Enlightenment*, pp. 150ff.
3. Sangharakshita, Bhikshu, *A Survey of Buddhism*, p. 452.
4. *Ibid.*, p. 454.
5. Śāntideva, p. 154.
6. Sangharakshita, p. 460.
7. *Bodhisattvabhūmi*, Fol. 6A, 2.2 to 3.1.
8. Śāntideva, p. 202.
9. *Ibid.*, p. 204.
10. *Ibid.*, p. 206.
11. *Ibid.*, p. 209.
12. *Ibid.*, pp. 162, 163, 164.
13. *Ibid.*, p. 159.
14. *Ibid.*, p. 168.
15. As quoted by Sangharakshita, p. 470.
16. Govinda, Lama Anagarika, *Ibid.*, pp. 243-4.
17. As quoted by Sangharakshita, p. 471.
18. Dayal, Har, *Bodhisattva Doctrine in Buddhist Sanskrit*

Literature, pp. 175-6.

19. *Pañcvimsatisahaśrikā*, 263-264. As quoted by Sangharakshita, pp. 476-7.
20. *Vajracchedikā*, Tr. Conze, p. 54.
21. Sangharakashita, pp. 480-1.
22. Śāntideva, p. 173.
23. *Ibid.*, p. 174.
24. *Ibid.*, pp. 176, 177, 178-9.
25. *Ibid.*, p. 181.
26. *Ibid.*, p. 182.
27. *Ibid.*, p. 183.
28. *Ibid.*, p. 186.
29. *Ibid.*, p. 188.
30. *Ibid.*, pp. 190-1.
31. *Ibid.*, p. 192.
32. *Vajracchedikā*, Tr. Conze, p. 25.

Chapter Eleven: The Buddhist Concept of Evil

1. Ling. T. O., *Buddhism and the Mythology of Evil*, p. 46.
2. Windisch, E., *Mara and Buddha*, p. 197. As referred to by Ling, p. 46.
3. Eliot, Sir Charles, *Hinduism and Buddhism*, Vol. 1. As referred to by Ling, p. 46.
4. *S.* III. 74.
5. *Loc. Cit.*
6. *Ibid.*, III. 38.
7. *Sn.* 436-439.
8. *Ibid.*, 1103.
9. *S.* III. 114.
10. Ling, p. 50.
11. *D.* III. 58.
12. *Ibid.*, I. 22.
13. Ling, p. 67.
14. *Ibid.*, p. 68.
15. *S.* IV. 306.
16. Śāntideva, p. 182.

Chapter Twelve: The Nature of Nirvana

1. Silva, Padmasiri de., pp. 49-70.

2. Nyanaponika Thera, *The Heart of Buddhist Meditation.* An excellent practical guide book to Buddhist meditation is *The Experience of Insight,* by Joseph Goldstein, Santa Cruz; Unity Press, 1976.

3. *M.* I. 111, Ñāṇananda, pp. 5-6.

4. Ñāṇananda, p. 6.

5. *Sn.* 757, Ñāṇananda, p. 29.

6. *Sn.* 8.

7. *Sn.* 916.

8. *S.* I. 202.

9. *Minor Anthologies of the Pali Canon,* SBB II, p. 10.

10. *Sn.* 734, 735; A. I. 236, S. III. 61; D. I. 223.

11. *U.* 80-1.

12. Conze, Edward, *Buddhist Thought in India,* p. 221.

13. *Ibid.*, p. 233.

14. Sangharakshita, p. 280.

15. *Prajñāpārmitāhṛdaya Sutra,* Tr. Edward Conze, *Buddhist Wisdom Books,* p. 81.

16. Nāgārjuna, *Mūla Mādhyamika Kārika,* Chap. XXV. 19.

17. Śāntideva, p. 214.

18. *The Holy Teaching of Vimalakīrti,* Tr. Robert A. F. Thurman, p. 24.

19. *Ibid.*, pp. 65-66.

20. *Ibid.*, p. 47.

21. *Ibid.*, p. 26.

22. *Ibid.*, p. 64.

23. *Ibid.*, p. 65.

Appendix: Buddhism and the Modern World

1. Gordon Rattray Taylor, *The Doomsday Book,* p. 16.

2. *Ibid.*, p. 23.

3. Desmond Morris, *The Human Zoo.*

4. Vance Packard, *A Nation of Strangers.*

5. *Sn.* 149.

6. *J.* I., 175ff.

7. *Ekindriyā manussā jīvasaññino rukkhasmiṃ*, Vinaya, IV, 34.

8. *Vinaya*, IV, 32-33.

9. Konrad Lorenz, *King Solomon's Ring.*

10. Konrad Lorenz, *Studies in Animal and Human Behavior*, vol. I & II, 1971. Konrad Lorenz, *Man Meets Dog.* Niko Tinbergen, *Curious Naturalists.*

11. Robert Ardrey, *The Social Contract*, pp. 91-92.

12. Robert Ardrey, *The Territorial Imperative.*

13. Konrad Lorenz, *On Aggression*, p. 40.

14. Robert Ardrey, *African Genesis*, pp. 86-89.

15. Anthony Storr, *Human Aggression*, pp. 27-37.

16. Lorenz, pp. 48-86.

17. Silva, Padmasiri de, p. 58.

18. *Vsm.* 470.

19. *Taṇhaṃ Nissāya taṇhā pahātabbā mānaṃ nissāya māno pahātabbo. A.* II, 145-146.

20. For a detailed discussion about the Buddhist theory of concept and reality, see: Bhikkhu Ñāṇananda, *Concept and Reality.*

21. *Saṃkappehi pareto so. Sn.* 818.

22. *Saṃkappa rāgo purisassa kāmo. S.* I, 22.

23. *M.* I, iff.

24. I am grateful to Dr. Parakrama Fernando for this example and for the valuable discussions I had with him on the idea of self.

25. *Na diṭṭhiyā na sutiyā na ñaṇena . . . suddhimāha, Sn* 839.

26. *Sn.* 1107; S. II, 119, Gunapala Dharmasiri, *A Buddhist Critique of the Christian Concept of God*, p. 174.

27. Silva, Padmasiri de, pp. 49-70.

28. Robert Ardrey, *The Social Contract*, pp. 367-368.

29. *S.* V, 272.

30. Gunapala Dharmasiri, *Ibid.*, p. 89.

31. Anthony Storr, pp. 76-77.

32. *Ibid.*, p. 76.

33. Victor E. Frankl, *Psychotherapy and Existentialism*, p. 80.

34. Erich Fromm, 'De-repression and Enlightenment,' in *Zen Buddhism and Psychoanalysis*, Eds., D. T. Suzuki, Erich Fromm, Richard de Martino, pp. 121-141.

Bibliography

A. PALI TEXTS AND TRANSLATIONS

1. *Aṅguttara Nikāya*, Eds. R. Morris and E. Hardy, 5 Vols., London: PTS, 1885-1900. Trs. F.L. Woodward and E.M. Hare, *The Book of the Gradual Sayings*, 5 Vols., London: PTS, 1931-1936.

2. *Dhammapada*, Ed. S. Sumangala Thero, London: PTS, 1914.

3. *Dīgha Nikāya*, Eds. T.W. Rhys Davids and J. E. Carpenter, 3 Vols., Dialogues of the Buddha, SBB, Vols. 2, 3 and 4, London: O.U.P., 1899-1921.

4. *Majjihima Nikāya*, Eds. V. Trenkner and R. Chalmers, 3 Vols., London: PTS, 1948-1951, Tr. I.B. Horner, *Middle Length Sayings*, 3 Vols., London: PTS, 1954-1959. *Majjihima Nikāya* in *Sutra Piṭaka*, Ed. Kirielle Gnanawimala thero, Ratnapura: Sastrodaya Press, 1960. *Majjihima Nikāya*, Ed. P.V. Bapat, Pali Publications: Bihar Government, 1958.

5. *Saṃyutta Nikāya*, Ed. L. Feer, 6 Vols., London: PTS, 1884-1904. Trs. C.A.F. Rhys Davids and F.L. Woodward, *The Book of the*

Kindred Sayings, 5 Vols., London: PTS, 1917-1930.

6. *Suttanipāta*, Eds. D. Anderson and H. Smith, London: PTS, 1948. Tr. V. Fausboll, SBE, Vol. 10, Part 2, Oxford, 1881.

7. *Thera-* and *Therigāthā*, Eds. H. Oldenberg and R. Pischel, London: PTS, 1883. Tr. C.A.F. Rhys Davids, *Psalms of the Early Buddhists*, 2 Vols., London: PTS, 1903-1913.

8. *Udāna*, Ed. P. Steinthal, London: PTS, 1904.

9. *Visuddhimagga* by Buddhaghosa, Ed. C.A.F. Rhys Davids, 2 Vols., London: PTS, 1920-1921. Tr. Bhikkhu Nyanamoli, *The Path of Purification*, A. Semage, Colombo, 1964.

B. MONOGRAPHS

1. Aronson, H., *Love and Sympathy in Theravada Buddhism*, Delhi: Matilal Banaransidas, 1980.

2. Ardrey, Robert, *African Genesis*, London: Collins, 1973.

3. Ardrey, Robert, *The Social Contract*, London: Collins, 1972.

4. Ardrey, Robert, *The Territorial Imperative*, London: Collins, 1967.

5. Buhler, G., Tr., *The Laws of Manu (Sacred Books of the East)*, Vol. XXV.

6.Conze, Edward, *Buddhist Thought in India*, London: Allen & Urwin, 1962.

7. Conze, Edward, Tr., *Pañcaviṃsatisāhaśrikā*, Buddhist Texts through the Ages, Oxford: Clarendon Press, 1954.

8. Conze, Edward, Tr., *Prajñāpārmitāhṛdaya Sūtra (Buddhist Wisdom Books)*, London: Allen & Urwin, 1970.

9. Conze, Edward, Tr., *Vajracchedikā Prajñāpāramitā (Buddhist Wisdom Books)*, London: Allen & Urwin, 1979.

10. Cook, Francis, H., *Hua-yen Buddhism*, The Pennsylvania State University Press, 1977.

11. Dayal, Har, *Bodhisattva Doctrine in Buddhist Sanskrit Literature*, London Kegan Paul, 1932.

12. De, Gokuldas, *Democracy in Early Buddhist Sanga*, Calcutta: Calcutta University Press, 1955.

13. Dharmasiri, Gunapala, *A Buddhist Critique of the Christian Concept of God*, U.S.A.: Golden Leaves Publishing, 1988.

14. Eliot, Sir Charles, *Hinduism and Buddhism*, Vol. 1, London: Arnold, 1921.

15. Frankl, Victor E., *Psychotherapy and Existentialism*, Harmondsworth: Pelican Books, 1973.

16. Fromm, Erich, "De-repression and Enlightenment,' in *Zen Buddhism and Psychoanalysis*, Suzuki, D.T., Erich Fromm, Richard De Martino, Eds., London: Allen & Urwin, 1960.

17. Ghurye, G.S., *Caste and Race in India*, London: Kegan Paul, 1932.

18. Goldstein, Joseph, *The Experience of Insight*, Santa Cruz: Unity Press, 1976.

19. Govinda, Lama Anagarika, "Origins of the Bodhisattva Ideal,' *Stepping Stones*, Vol. II, January 1952.

20. Jayatilleke, K.N., *Early Buddhist Theory of Knowledge*, London: 1963.

21. Jayatilleke, K.N., *Survival and Karma in Buddhist Perspective*, Kandy: BPS, 1972.

22. Jayatilleke, K.N., *Ethics in Buddhist Perspective*, Kandy: B.P.S., 1972.

23. Joshi, Lal Mani, *Discerning the Buddha*, Delhi: Munshiram Manoharlal, 1983.

24. Katz, Nathan, Ed., *Buddhism and Western Philosophy*, Delhi: Sterling Press, 1981.

25. Ling, T.O., *Buddhism and the Mythology of Evil*, London: Allen & Urwin, 1962.

26. Lorenz, Konrad, *King Solomon's Ring*, London: Pan Books, 1953.

27. Lorenz, Konrad, *Man Meets Dog*, Harmondsworth: Penguin Books, 1974.

28. Lorenz, Konrad, *On Aggression*, U.S.A.: Bantam Books, 1971.

29. Lorenz, Konrad, *Studies in Animal and Human Behavior*, London: Methuen Books, Vol. I & II, 1971.

30. Malalasekara, G.P. and K.N . Jayatilleke, *Buddhism and the Race Question*, Paris: UNESCO, 1958.

31. Marion, L., Tr., *Entering the Path of Enlightenment* (Santideva, *Bodhicaryāvatāra*), London: Macmillan, 1971.

32. Moody, Raymond, *Life and Life*, New York: Bantam Books, 1976.

33. Morris, Desmond, *The Human Zoo*, London: Corgi books, 1971.

34. Nagley, Winfield E., *Philosophy East and West*, Moore Memorial Volume, Vol. XVII, no. 1-4, 1967.

35. Nyanamoli, Bhikkhy, Tr., *The Pāṭimokkha*, Bangkok: Social Science Association, 1966.

36. *Ñāṇānanda*, Bhikkhu, Tr., *Concept and Reality*, Kandy: Buddhist Publication Society, 1971.

37. Nyanaponika, Thera, *The Heart of Buddhist Meditation*, London: Rider, 1969.

38. Packard, Vance, *A Nation of Strangers*, U.S.A.: Pocket books, 1974.

39. Piyadassi, Thera, Tr., *The Book of Protection*, Kandy: BPS, 1975.

40. Piyadassi, Thera, Ed., *Narada Felicitation Volume*, Kandy: BPS, 1979.

41. Rodney, Jonathan, *Explorations of a Hypnotist*, London: Elek Books, 1959.

42. Sangharakshita, Bhikkhu, *A Survey of Buddhism*, Bangalore: Indian Institute of World Culture, 1966.

43. Silva, Padmasiri de, *Buddhist and Freudian Psychology*, Colombo: Lake House Investments, 1973.

44. Stevenson, Ian, *Twenty Cases Suggestive of Reincarnation*, New York: Proceedings of the American Society for Psychological Research, Vol. XXVI, Sept., 1966.

45. Storr, Anthony, *Human Aggression*, Harmondsworth: Pelican Books, 1970.

46. Taylor, Gordon Rattray, *The Doomsday Book*, London: Thames and Hudson, 1970.

47. Thurman, Robert A.F., Tr., *The Holy Teaching of Vimalakirti*, Pennsylvania State University Press, 1976.

48. Tinbergen, Niko, *Curious Naturalists*, Harmondsworth: Penguin Books, 1974.

49. Wentz, Evans, Tr., *Tibetan Book of the Dead*, Oxford: Clarendon Press, 1957.

50. Windisch, E., *Māra and Buddha*, Leipzig, 1895.

Index